The Gig Book

Acoustic Hits

Published by
Wise Publications
14-15 Berners Street,
London W1T 3LJ, UK.

Exclusive Distributors:
Music Sales Limited
Distribution Centre,
Newmarket Road, Bury St Edmunds,
Suffolk IP33 3YB, UK.
Music Sales Pty Limited
20 Resolution Drive, Caringbah,
NSW 2229, Australia.

Order No. AM997326
ISBN 978-1-84938-078-2

Compiled by Nick Crispin.
Text by Graham Vickers.
Picture research by Jacqui Black.
All photographs courtesy of LFI,
except page 7 (Rex Features) and
page 95 (Redferns).
Music engraved by Paul Ewers Music Design.
Edited by Tom Farncombe and Adrian Hopkins.
Design by Fresh Lemon.

www.musicsales.com

Printed in Thailand.

Wise Publications
part of The Music Sales Group
London / New York / Paris / Sydney / Copenhagen / Berlin / Tokyo / Madrid

The GigBook Acoustic Hits

Introduction

Perhaps the golden age of popular acoustic music was the 1960s when the lone singer/songwriter equipped with an acoustic guitar became associated with a new and more personal type of song.

Bob Dylan, Leonard Cohen, Donovan, Cat Stevens and Paul Simon all established their individual styles with mainly acoustic recordings. Joni Mitchell, pictured right, complicated the trend, often playing her acoustic guitar in a variety of unguessable tunings that sometimes tested the loyalty of those fans who would try to emulate her by watching her fingers; somehow it only made her work sound even more personal.

Eventually most of the acoustic pioneers embraced more elaborate instrumentation and so the stage was set for the occasional elective back-to-basics concert or recording. Strangely enough it may have been Elvis Presley—who generally sang other people's songs, nearly always with an electric band—who started the trend in 1968. The stripped-down, in-the-round acoustic jam session in *Elvis: The Comeback Special* reminded even hardcore fans just how great Presley really was. The Beatles' 1970 movie *Let It Be* featured several acoustic-based jam sessions and, in 1979, Pete Townshend—

for whom electricity might reasonably have been assumed to be a musical life-support system—performed an impressive acoustic version of 'Pinball Wizard' for a charity show.

By 1989 MTV had launched its *Unplugged* series so giving a rolling platform to rock musicians who wanted to revisit their unamplified days, and demonstrate that their songs could shine without layers of studio production. It also gave a trendy tag to any artists who might want to make acoustic-flavoured albums of their own. Among the many who have done so are Coldplay, U2 and Van Morrison.

Through it all, one thing hasn't changed. Anyone who wants to write a song can sit down with an acoustic guitar more or less anywhere and just do it. It may not result in a 'Bohemian Rhapsody', but it can produce intensely intimate songs like 'Both Sides Now', 'Vincent' or 'Songbird'. Now you can play them all...and maybe even write your own.

100
ACOUSTIC
SONGS

Angel

Words & Music by Sarah McLachlan

Verse 2:
So tired of the straight line
And everywhere you turn, there's vultures and thieves at your back.
The storm keeps on twisting,
You keep on building the lies that you make up for all that you lack.
It don't make no difference, escape one last time,
It's easier to believe in this sweet madness,
Oh, this glorious sadness that brings me to my knees.

In the arms of the angels...

Angels

Words & Music by Robbie Williams & Guy Chambers

she of - fers me___ pro-tec - tion, a lot of love and af - fec-

- tion whe-ther I'm right or wrong. And down the wa - ter-fall___

___ wher-ev - er it___ may take___ me, I know that life___won't break___

___ me,___ when I come___ to call, she won't for - sake

___ me, I'm lov - ing an - gels in - stead.

2. When I'm feel-ing weak___ and my pain___ walks down___ a one-

- way street, I look a-bove and I know___

I'll al - ways be blessed with love, and
as the feel-ing grows she brings flesh to my bones, and
when love is dead, I'm lov-ing an-gels in-stead. And through it all

D.S. al Coda

Coda E/G♯

And through it all she of - fers me pro-tec -
- tion, a lot of love and af-fec - tion whe-ther I'm right or wrong. And down the wa - ter-fall
wher-ev-er it may take me, I know that life won't break me, when I come to call,
she won't for-sake me, I'm lov-ing an-gels in-stead.

13

Angie

Words & Music by Mick Jagger & Keith Richards

♩ = 70

1. Oh An - gie,___ oh An - gie,___
(Verses 2 & 3 see block lyrics)
when will those dark clouds dis - ap - pear?___

An - gie,___ An - gie,___ where will it lead us from
(Verse 4 (𝄌) see block lyrics)
here?___ With no lov-ing in our souls and no mon-ey in our coats,___
you can't say__ we're sat-is - fied.___ But An - gie,___

To Coda ⊕

D.S. al Coda
(after 2 repeats)

An - gie, you can't say__ we've nev-er tried.___

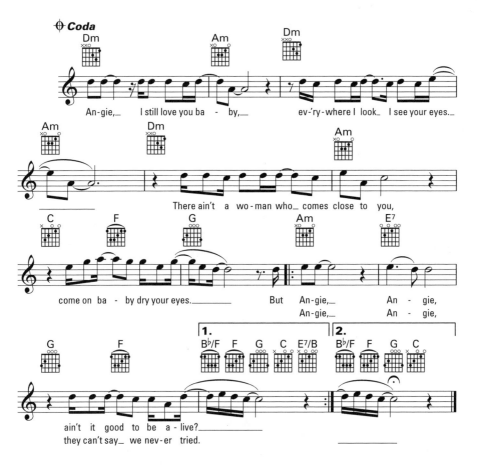

◇ Coda

An-gie,— I still love you ba - by,— ev-'ry-where I look— I see your eyes.—

There ain't a wo-man who— comes close to you,

come on ba - by dry your eyes._____ But An-gie,— An - gie,

An-gie,— An - gie,

1.
ain't it good to be a - live?_____

they can't say— we nev-er tried. _____

2.

Verse 2:
Angie you're beautiful, but ain't it time we said goodbye?
Angie I still love you, remember all those nights we cried?
All the dreams we held so close, seemed to all go up in smoke
Let me whisper in your ear, "Angie, Angie, where will it lead us from here?"

Verse 3:
Instrumental for 8 bars
Oh Angie don't you weep, ah, your kisses still taste sweet
I hate that sadness in your eyes
But Angie, Angie, ain't it time we said goodbye?

Verse 4 (𝄌):
Instrumental for 4 bars
With no loving in our souls and no money in our coats
You can't say we're satisfied.
But Angie... (Coda)

15

Babylon

Words & Music by David Gray

2. Sat - ur - day,_ I'm run - nin' wild,_ an' all_ the lights are chang - in' red_

(Verse 3 see block lyrics)

_ to green. Mov - in' through the clouds, I'm push - in',

che - mi - cals are rush - in' in_ my_ blood - stream. On - ly wish_

_ that you_ were here, you know I'm seein'_ it so_ clear,_ I've_ been a -

- fraid_ to show_ you how_ I real - ly feel,_ ad - mit_

_ to some of these_ bad mis - takes I've_ made.

An' if you want it____ come an' get____ it,____

for cry-in' out____ loud.____ The love that I____ was

giv-in' you____ was____ nev-er in_____ doubt.____

Let go your heart,____ let go your head____ and feel it____ now.

Let go your heart____ let go your head____ and feel it____ now,____

1.

Ba-by-lon,____ Ba-by-lon,____

Ba-by-lon.____

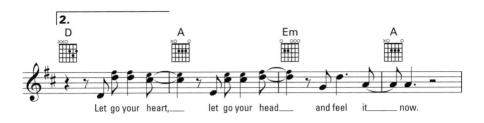

Let go your heart,___ let go your head___ and feel it___ now.

Let go your heart___ let go your head___ and feel it___ now.___

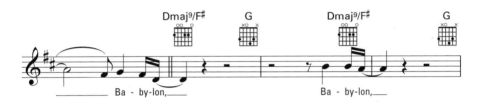

Ba - by-lon,___ Ba - by-lon,___

Ba - by - lon,___ Ba - by-lon.___

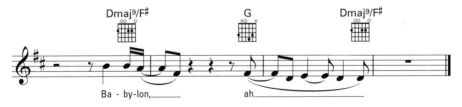

Ba - by-lon,___ ah.___

Verse 3:
Sunday, all the lights in London
Shining sky is fading red to blue
Kickin' through the autumn leaves
An' wonderin' where it is you might be going to
Turnin' back for home
You know I'm feeling so alone, I can't believe
Climbin' on the stair I turn around
To see you smiling there in front of me.

Boots Of Spanish Leather

Words & Music by Bob Dylan

♩=101

Capo fret 1

Oh I'm sail - in' a - way   my___ own true

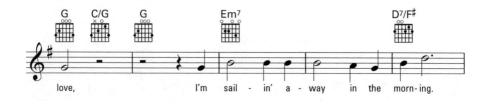

love,   I'm sail - in' a - way in the morn - ing.

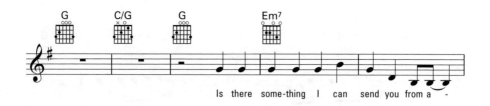

Is there some-thing I can send you from a -

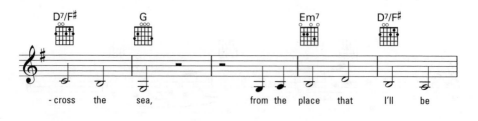

- cross the sea,   from the place that I'll be

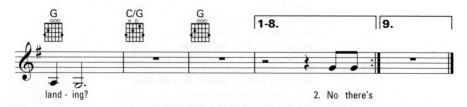

land - ing?   2. No there's

20

Verse 2:
No there's nothin' you can send me my own true love
There's nothin' I wish to be ownin'
Just carry yourself back to me unspoiled
From across that lonesome ocean.

Verse 3:
Oh, but I just thought you might long want something fine
Made of silver or of golden
Either from the mountains of Madrid
Or from the coast of Barcelona.

Verse 4:
Oh, but if I had the stars from the darkest night
And the diamonds from the deepest ocean
I'd forsake them all for your sweet kiss
For that's all I'm wishin' to be ownin'.

Verse 5:
That I might be gone a long time
And it's only that I'm askin'
Is there somethin' I can send you to remember me by
To make your time more easy passin'.

Verse 6:
Oh, how can, how can you ask me again
It only brings me sorrow
The same thing I want from you today
I would want again tomorrow.

Verse 7:
I got a letter on a lonesome day
It was from her ship a-sailin'
Saying I don't know when I'll be comin' back again
It depends on how I'm a-feelin'.

Verse 8:
Well, if you my love must think that-a-way
I'm sure your mind is roamin'
I'm sure your heart is not with me
But with the country to where you're goin'.

Verse 9:
So take heed, take heed of the western wind
Take heed of the stormy weather
And yes, there's something you can send back to me
Spanish boots of Spanish leather.

Both Sides Now

Words & Music by Joni Mitchell

♩ = 97

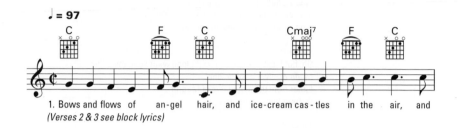

1. Bows and flows of an-gel hair, and ice-cream cas-tles in the air, and

(Verses 2 & 3 see block lyrics)

fea - ther can - yons ev-'ry-where, I've looked at clouds that way. But

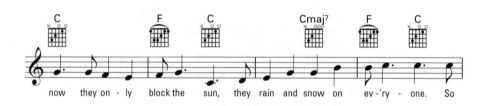

now they on - ly block the sun, they rain and snow on ev-'ry - one. So

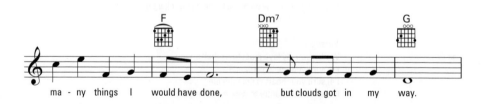

ma - ny things I would have done, but clouds got in my way.

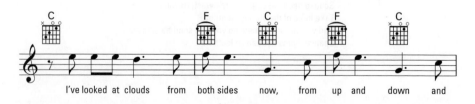

I've looked at clouds from both sides now, from up and down and

22

still some - how   it's cloud   il - lu - sions   I   re - call,   I   real - ly___ don't know

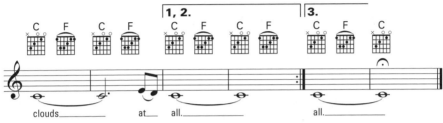

1, 2.   **3.**

clouds_____   at___ all._____   all._____

Verse 2:
Moons and Junes and Ferris wheels
The dizzy dancing way you feel
As every fairy tale comes real
I've looked at love that way
But now it's just another show
You leave 'em laughing when you go
And if you care don't let them know
Don't give yourself away
I've looked at love from both sides now
From give and take and still somehow
It's love's illusions I recall
I really don't know love at all.

Verse 3:
Tear and fears and feeling proud
To say "I love you" right out loud
Dreams and schemes and circus crowds
I've looked at life that way
But now old friends are acting strange
They shake their heads, they say I've changed
But something's lost but something's gained
In living every day
I've looked at life from both sides now
From win and lose and still somehow
It's life's illusions I recall
I really don't know life at all.

Black Velvet

Words & Music by Christopher Ward & David Tyson

Original key: E♭ minor (tune guitar down one tone)

1. Mis - sis - sip - pi   in the mid - dle of a   dry___ spell,___
(Verse 2 see block lyrics)

Jim-my Rog - ers___ on the Vic-tro-la up high,___   Ma-ma's danc - ing___with a

ba - by___ on her shoul-der,___   the sun is set-ting like_ mo - las - ses___ in the sky.___

The boy could sing,___   knew_ how to   move   ev - 'ry - thing.___

Al - ways want-ing   more,___   he'd leave you long-ing   for

Black Vel - vet and that   lit-tle boy's_ smile,___   Black Vel - vet with that

(Guitar solo)

Black Vel - vet and that lit - tle boy's__ smile, Black Vel - vet with that

1.
slow south-ern style, a new re - li - gion__ that-'ll bring you__ to your knees.

2.
Black Vel - vet,__ if__ you please.____ Black Vel - vet,__ if

Repeat ad lib. to fade

you please.__

Verse 2:
Up in Memphis the music's like a heatwave
White lightning, bound to drive you wild
Mama's ba-by's in the heart of ev'ry school girl
'Love Me Tender' leaves them crying in the aisle
The way he moved, it was a sin, so sweet and true
Always wanting more, he'd leave you longing for...

Bridge Over Troubled Water

Words & Music by Paul Simon

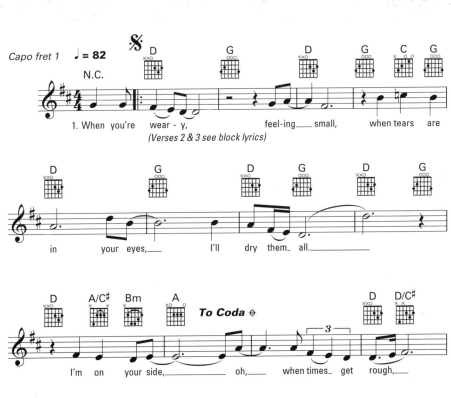

1. When you're wear - y, feel-ing___ small, when tears are
(Verses 2 & 3 see block lyrics)

in your eyes,___ I'll dry them___ all.___

I'm on your side,___ oh,___ when times___ get rough,___

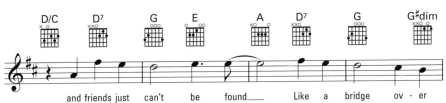

and friends just can't be found.___ Like a bridge ov - er

trou-bled wat - er I will lay me down, like a bridge ov - er

Verse 2:
When you're down and out, when you're on the street
When evening falls so hard I'll comfort you
I'll take your part oh, when darkness comes
And pain is all around.
Like a bridge over troubled water...

Verse 3:
Sail on silver girl, sail on by
Your time has come to shine, your dreams are on their way
See how they shine oh, when you need a friend
I'm sailing right behind.
Like a bridge over troubled water...

Brown Eyed Girl

Words & Music by Van Morrison

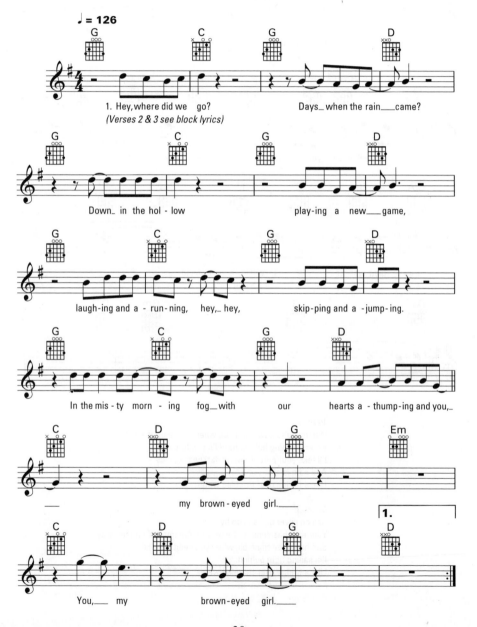

♩ = 126

1. Hey, where did we go? Days_ when the rain___ came?
(Verses 2 & 3 see block lyrics)

Down_ in the hol - low playing a new___ game,

laugh-ing and a - run - ning, hey,_ hey, skip-ping and a -jump-ing.

In the mis - ty morn - ing fog_with our hearts a - thump-ing and you,_

___ my brown - eyed girl.___

1.

You,___ my brown-eyed girl.___

2, 3.

Do you___ re - mem - ber when   we used to sing,___

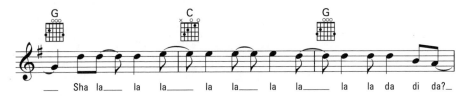

___ Sha la___ la la___ la la___ la la___ la la da di da?___

___ Sha la___ la la___ la la___ la la___

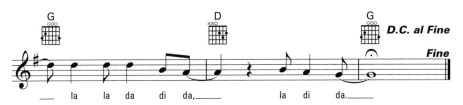

D.C. al Fine

Fine

___ la la da di da,___ la di da.___

Verse 2:
Whatever happened to Tuesday and so slow?
Going down to the old mine with a transistor radio.
Standing in the sunlight, laughing,
Hide behind a rainbow's wall.
Slipping and a sliding
All along the waterfall with you,
My brown-eyed girl.
You, my brown-eyed girl.

Verse 3:
So hard to find my way, now that I'm on my own.
Saw you just the other day, my, how you have grown!
Cast my mem'ry back there,
Lord, sometimes I'm overcome thinking about
Making love in the green grass,
Behind the stadium with you,
My brown-eyed girl.
You, my brown-eyed girl.

31

Bye Bye Love

Written by the exotically-named husband and wife team Diadorius Boudleaux Bryant and Matilda Genevieve Scaduto (a.k.a. Boudleaux & Felice Bryant) 'Bye Bye Love' was both a perfect pop song and a career-launching number for The Everly Brothers on Cadence Records in 1957. Despite being surrounded by great session guitarists Chet Atkins, Hank Garland and Ray Edenton, The Everlys themselves played the rich chiming acoustic guitars that gave 'Bye Bye Love' and several subsequent hits such a distinctive sound. Three years after the success of 'Bye Bye Love' launched Archie Bleyer's modest Cadence label into the big time the Everlys would repeat the trick by kick-starting the singles output of the new album-oriented Warner Bros. record label. This time the song was their own 'Cathy's Clown' (Page 37) and it would sell eight million copies worldwide.

The Gig Book
The Everly Brothers

Bye Bye Love

Words & Music by Felice Bryant & Boudleaux Bryant

33

California Dreamin'

Words & Music by John Phillips & Michelle Phillips

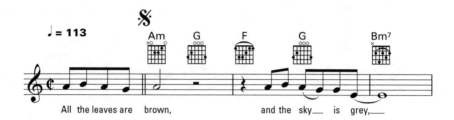

All the leaves are brown, and the sky__ is grey,__

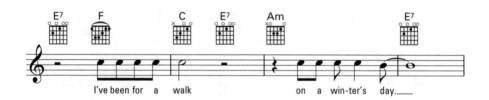

I've been for a walk on a win-ter's day.__

1. I'd be safe and warm,__ if I was in L. A.__
2. If I did-n't tell, her,__ I could leave to-day.__

To Coda ⊕

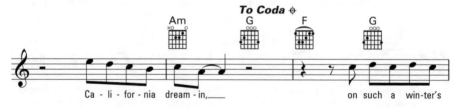

Ca - li - for - nia dream - in, on such a win-ter's

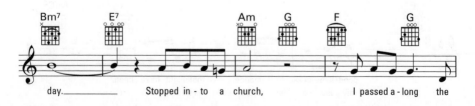

day.__ Stopped in - to a church, I passed a - long the

way. Oh, I got down on my knees,

and I pre-tend to pray.

You know the preach-er likes the

cold, he knows I'm gon-na stay

Ca-li-for-nia

dream-in'

on such a win-ter's day.

D.S. al Coda

All the leaves are

Coda

on such a win-ter's day.

On such a win-ter's day.

On such a win-ter's day.

35

Candle In The Wind

Words & Music by Elton John & Bernie Taupin

♩ = 63

1. Good-bye Nor - ma Jean____ though I nev-er knew you at all____
(Verse 2 see block lyrics)

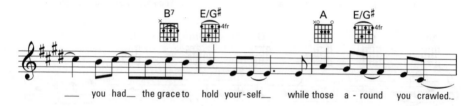

____ you had____ the grace to hold your-self____ while those a - round you crawled..

____ They crawled out of the wood - work____

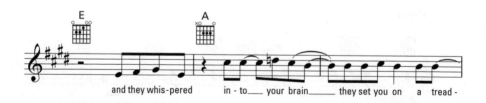

and they whis-pered in - to____ your brain____ they set you on a tread -

- mill____ and they made you change your name.____

And it seems to me you lived your life___ like a

can - dle in___ the wind,___ nev - er know - ing___ who to cling

___ to___ when the rain___ set in,___ and I

would have liked___ to have known___ you but___ I was just___

___ a kid,___ your can-dle had burned out long___ be - fore___ your

le - gend ev - er did.___

Verse 2:
Loneliness was tough
The toughest role you ever played
Hollywood created a superstar
And pain was the price you paid
Even when you died
Oh the press still hounded you
All the papers had to say
Was that Marilyn was found in the nude.

Cathy's Clown

Words & Music by Don Everly

♩ = 120

Don't want your love_____ a - ny - more,

don't want your kiss - - es that's for sure. I die each

time_____ I hear this sound. Here he comes,_____

To Coda ✛

_____ that's Ca - thy's clown._____ 1. I've got to stand tall,_____ you know a man can't
(Verse 2 see block lyric)

crawl. For when he knows you tell lies and he lets them pass by, then he's not a man at

D.S. al Coda

all._____ Don't want your

Coda ✛

Repeat to fade

clown._____ that's Ca - thy's

Verse 2:
When you see me shed a tear
And you know that it's sincere
Don't you think it's kind of sad
That you're treating me so bad
Or don't you even care?

The Closest Thing To Crazy

Words & Music by Mike Batt

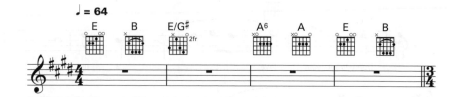

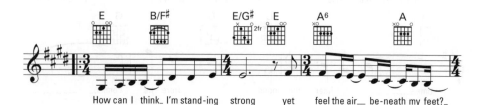

How can I think_ I'm stand-ing strong yet feel the air_ be-neath my feet?_

How can hap - pi-ness feel so wrong?

How can mi - se-ry feel_ so sweet? How can you let_ me watch you

sleep then break my dreams the way_ you do?____

40

How can I____ have got in so deep?

Why did I____ fall in love with you? This is the

clos - est thing_ to cra - zy I have ev - er been._ Feel - ing

twen - ty two,__ act - ing sev - en - teen._ This is the

near - est thing_ to cra - zy I have ev - er known. I was

nev - er cra - zy on my own__ and

now I know that there's a link be - tween the two.____

41

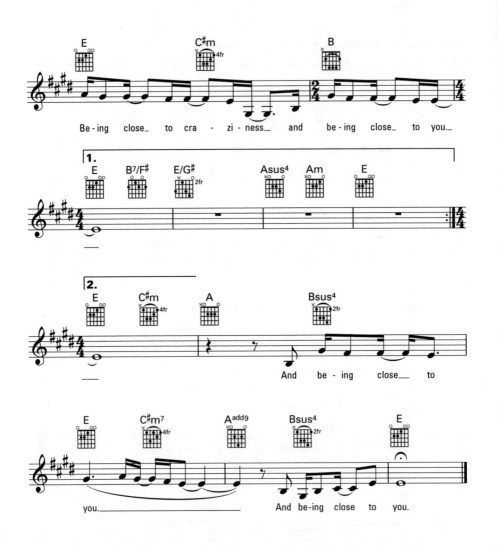

Be - ing close_ to cra - zi - ness_ and be - ing close_ to you._

1.

2.

And be - ing close_ to

you._____ And be-ing close to you.

Verse 2:
How can you make me fall apart
Then break my fall with loving lies?
It's so easy to break a heart
It's so easy to close your eyes
How can you treat me like a child
Yet like a child I yearn for you?
How can anyone feel so wild?
How can anyone feel so blue.

Cracklin' Rosie

Words & Music by Neil Diamond

♩ = 128

Capo fret 1   N.C.

Crack-lin' Ro-sie, get on board.___ We're gon-na ride___ till there ain't

___ no more___ to go, tak-in' it slow.___ And Lord don't you

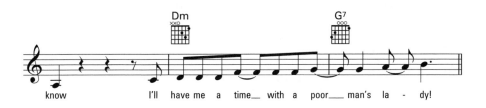

know I'll have me a time___ with a poor___ man's la - dy!

Hitch-in' on a twi-light train,___ ain't no-thing here___ that I care___
Crack-lin' Ro-sie make me smile,___ and girl if it lasts___ for an hour.___

43

to take_ a - long, may - be a song_
that's all - right. We got all night_

to sing when I want._ Don't need to say please to no man_
to set the world right._ Find us a dream_ that don't ask_

_ for a hap - py tune._
_ no ques - tions, yeah._ Oh I love my_

_ Ro-sie child. You got the way to make_ me hap - py, You and me, we go_

_ in style._ Crack-'l - in' Rose, you're a store - bought wo-man, but

you make me feel_ like a gui - tar hum - min'. So hang on to me,_ girl, our song_

Constant Craving

Words & Music by K.D. Lang & Ben Mink

1. Ev - en through the dark - est phase, be it thick or

(Verse 2 see block lyric)

(D.S. Instrumental)

thin.___ Al - ways some-one march - es brave,

here be - neath my skin.___ *mf* And con - stant

crav - ing has al - ways___ been.

Verse 2:
Maybe a great magnet
Pull all souls towards truth,
Or maybe it is life itself
That feeds wisdom to its youth.

Dear Prudence

Words & Music by John Lennon & Paul McCartney

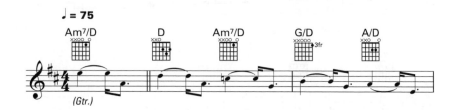

(Gtr.)

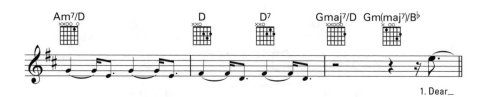

1. Dear__

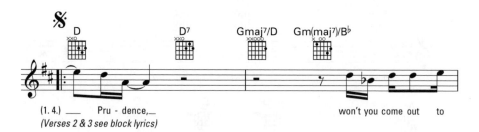

(1. 4.) __ Pru - dence,__ won't you come out to
(Verses 2 & 3 see block lyrics)

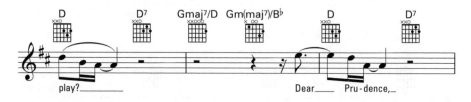

play?_____ Dear__ Pru - dence,__

greet the brand new day._____

48

49

- round.

3. Dear___

Coda

sun is up,___ the sky is blue,___ it's

beau - ti - ful,___ and so are you.___ Dear

Pru - dence,___ won't you come out to play?___

Fade to end

(Gtr.)

Verse 2:
Dear Prudence, open up your eyes
Dear Prudence, see the sunny skies
The wind is low, the birds will sing
That you are part of ev'rything
Dear Prudence, won't you open up your eyes?

Verse 3:
Dear Prudence, let me see you smile
Dear Prudence, like a little child
The clouds will be a daisy chain
So let me see you smile again
Dear Prudence, won't you let me see you smile?

Diamonds And Rust

Words & Music by Joan Baez

♩ = 65

1. Well, I'll be_ damned, here comes_ your

ghost a - gain,_ but that's not un - us - u - al._ It's just that the

moon is full,_ and you hap - pened_ to call. And

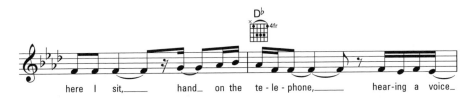

here I sit,_ hand_ on the te - le - phone,_ hear-ing a voice_

_ I'd known_ a cou-ple of light_ years a - go,_ head-ing straight for a

_____ you stand-ing with brown leaves fall-ing all a-round and snow in your hair. Now you're smil-

- ing out the win-dow of that crum-my ho-tel o - ver Wa - shing-ton Square. Our breath_

_____comes out, white clouds, ming-les and hangs in the air.____ Speak-ing

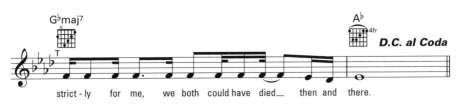

strict - ly for me, we both could have died__ then and there.

Verse 2:
Well, you burst on the scene already a legend
The unwashed phenomenon
The original vagabond
You strayed into my arms
And there you stayed
Temporarily lost at sea
The madonna was yours for free
Yes, the girl on the half-shell
Could keep you unharmed.

Verse 3:
Now you're telling me you're not nostalgic
Then give me another word for it
You who are so good with words
And at keeping things vague.
'Cause I need some of that vagueness now
It's all come back too clearly
Yes I loved you dearly
And if you're offering me diamonds and rust
I've already paid.

Dream Catch Me

Words & Music by Crispin Hunt, Gordon Mills & Newton Faulkner

54

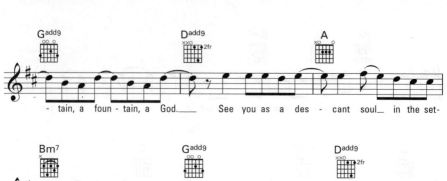

-tain, a foun-tain, a God.___ See you as a des - cant soul___ in the set-

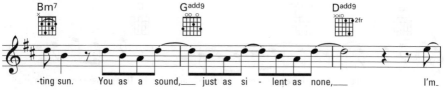

-ting sun. You as a sound,___ just as si - lent as none,___ I'm___

___ yours._____ There's a place I go___ when I'm a - lone,___

___ do an-y-thing I want,___ be an-y-one I wan - na be. But it is us___

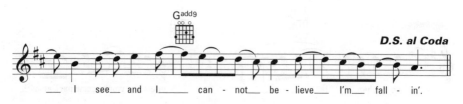

___ I see___ and I___ can - not___ be - lieve___ I'm___ fall - in'.

_____ or else I won't come back at all.___

56

Don't Dream It's Over

Words & Music by Neil Finn

Capo fret 1　♩ = **80**

1. There is free-dom with-in,　there is free-dom with-out,
(Verses 2 & 3 see block lyrics)

try to catch the de - luge in a pa - per cup.

There's a bat-tle a - head,　ma-ny bat-tles are lost,

but you'll ne-ver see the end of the road_ while you're trav-'ling with me._

Hey now,_ hey_ now,_ don't dream it's o - ver.

Hey now,_ hey_ now_ when the world comes in,_ they_

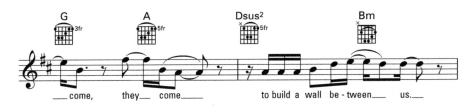

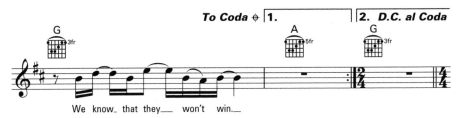

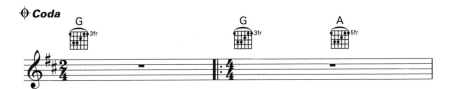

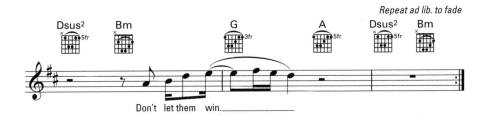

Verse 2:
Now I'm towing my car, there's a hole in the roof
My possessions are causing me suspicion but there's no proof
In the paper today tales of war and of waste
But you turn right over to the T.V. page.

Hey now,...

Verse 3:
Now I'm walking again to the beat of a drum
And I'm counting the steps to the door of your heart
Only shadows ahead barely clearing the roof
Get to know the feeling of liberation and release.

Hey now,...

Don't Know Why

Words & Music by Jesse Harris

Verse 3:
Out across the endless sea
I will die in ecstacy
But I'll be a bag of bones
Driving down the road alone
My heart is drenched in wine
But you'll be on my mind forever.

Verse 4:
Something has to make you run
I don't know why I didn't come
I feel as empty as a drum
I don't know why I didn't come
I don't know why I didn't come.

Everybody's Talkin'

Words & Music by Fred Neil

go-in'_ where the wea-ther suits my clothes._

Back-in' off of the north-east winds,_ sail - in' on_ sum-mer breeze._

_ And skip-pin' ov - er the o - cean like a stone._

To Coda ⊕

Woh, woh, woh, woh, woh, woh, woh, woh, woh, woh,

D.S. al Coda

woh, woh, woh,_ woh,_

⊕ **Coda**

Ev - 'ry - bo-dy's talk - in' at_ me._

Ah._

63

Everything I Own

Words & Music by David Gates

66

Father And Son

Words & Music by Cat Stevens

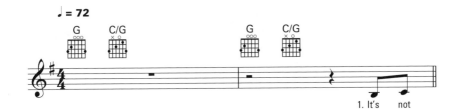

1. It's not

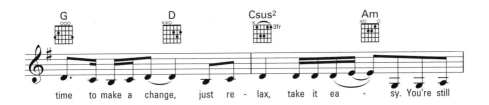

time to make a change, just re - lax, take it ea - sy. You're still

young, that's your fault,__ there's so much you have__ to know. Find__ a girl,__

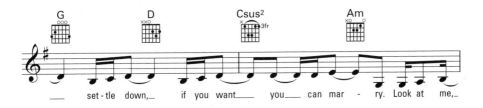

__ set - tle down,__ if you want__ you__ can mar - ry. Look at me,__

__ I am old__ but I'm hap - py. (1. 3.) I was

once like you are now,__ and I know__ that it's__ not ea - sy__ to be calm__

_____ when you've found__ some-thing go-ing on.__ But take your time,__

__ think a lot,__ think of ev - 'ry-thing__ you've got,__ for you will

still be here__ to - mor - row,__ but your dreams may

not.

{ 2. How can I__
{ (Verse 4 see block lyrics)

__ try to ex - plain? When I do,__ he turns a-way__ a-gain. It's al-

Verse 4:
And all the times that I've cried
Keeping all the thing I knew inside
It's hard, but it's harder to ignore it
If they were right, I'd agree
But it's them they know, not me
Now there's a way
And I know I have to go away
I know I have to go.

Fairytale Of New York

Words & Music by Shane MacGowan & Jem Finer

1. It was Christ-mas Eve,__ babe, in the drunk tank, when an old man
(Verse 2 see block lyrics)

said to me,__ "Won't see a-noth-er one". And then he sang a song, "The rare old

moun-tain dew". I turned my face a-way, and dreamed a-bout you. 2. Got on a

dreams come true.

3. They got

cars big as bars, they got riv-ers of gold, but the wind goes right through you, it's no

place for the old,___ when you first took my hand on a cold___ Christ-mas Eve, you

pro-mised me Broad-way was wait-ing for me.___ 4. You were

hand-some, you were pret-ty, Queen of New York Ci-ty. When the band fin-ished play-ing, they
(Verse 5 see block lyric)

howled out for more. Sin - at -ra was swing-ing, all the drunks, they were sing-ing. We

kissed on the cor - ner, then danced through the night.___ The

boys of the N. Y. P. D. choir___ were sing-ing,___ "Gal - way

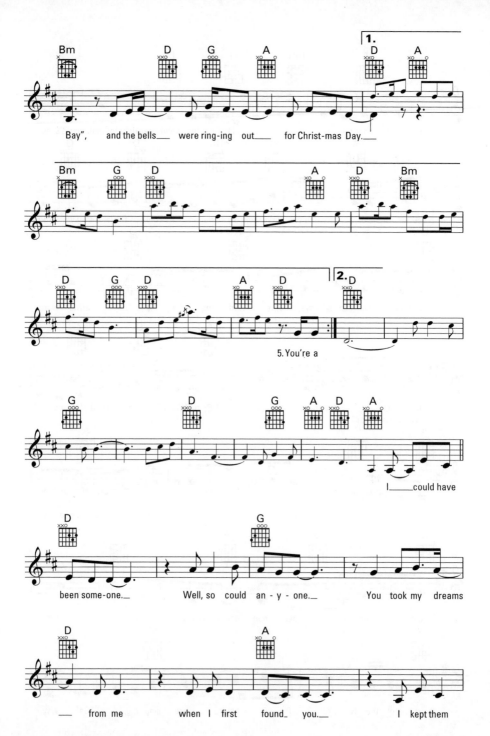

Bay", and the bells___ were ring-ing out___ for Christ-mas Day.___

5. You're a

I___could have

been some-one.___ Well, so could an-y-one.___ You took my dreams

___ from me when I first found_ you.___ I kept them

72

with me, babe,— I put them with my own.— Can't— make it

all a-lone,— I've built my dreams a-round you. The

boys of the N. Y. P. D. choir— still sing-ing— "Gal-way

Bay", and the bells— are ring-ing out— for Christ-mas Day.—

Verse 2:
Got on a lucky one
Came in eighteen-to-one
I've got a feeling
This one's for me and you
So happy Christmas
I love you baby
I can see a better time
When all our dreams come true.

Verse 5:
You're a bum. You're a punk. You're an old slut on junk
Lying there almost dead on a drip in that bed
You scum-bag, you maggot, you cheap lousy faggot
Happy Christmas, your arse, I pray God it's our last.

Fields Of Gold

Words & Music by Sting

74

Verse 2:
So she took her love for to gaze a-while upon the fields of barley
In his arms she fell, as her hair came down among the fields of gold.

Verse 3:
Will you stay with me? Will you be my love among the fields of barley?
We'll forget the sun in his jealous sky, as we lie in fields of gold.

Verse 4:
See the west wind move like a lover so upon the fields of barley
Feel her body rise when you kiss her mouth among the fields of gold.

50 Ways To Leave Your Lover

Words & Music by Paul Simon

back Jack, make a new plan, Stan, you don't need to be

coy, Roy, { just get your-self free. } Hop on the
{ just lis - ten to me. }

bus, Gus, you don't need to dis - cuss___ much,_____ just drop off the

1.

To Coda⊕
(last time)

key Lee, and get your-self free. Slip out the

2.

D.C. al Coda
(with repeats)

⊕ Coda

free. free.

Verse 2:
She said, "It grieves me now to see you in such pain
I wish there was somethin' I could do to make you smile again."
I said, "I appreciate that, and could you please explain
About the fifty ways?"
She said, "Why don't we both just sleep on it tonight
I'm sure in the morning you'll begin to see the light."
And then she kissed me and I realized she probably was right
There must be fifty ways to leave your lover
Fifty ways to leave your lover.

Just slip out the back Jack...

Fourth Time Around

Words & Music by Bob Dylan

1. When she said, "Don't waste___ your words, they're just___ lies,"___ I
(Verses 2-5 see block lyrics)

cried___ she was deaf.

And she worked on___ my face___ un-til break-ing___ my eyes,___ then said,

"What else___ you got left?" It___ was

then that I___ got up to leave___ but she said,___ "Don't fo-get,

ev - 'ry - bo - dy___ must give some-thing back___ for

some - thing___ they get." ___

4° *D.S. al Coda*

⊕ *Coda*

And I, I nev-er___ took much,__ I nev-er

asked for your_ crutch,___ now don't ask___ for mine.___

Verse 2:
I stood there and hummed, I tapped on her drum and asked her how come.
And she buttoned her boot and straightened her suit, then she said "Don't get cute."
So I forced my hands in my pockets and felt with my thumbs,
Gallantly handed her my very last piece of gum.

Verse 3:
She threw me outside, I stood in the dirt where ev'ryone walked.
And after finding I'd forgotten my shirt, I went back and knocked.
I waited in the hallway, she went to get it and I tried to make sense,
Out of that picture of you in your wheelchair that leaned up against...

Verse 4:
Her Jamaican rum and when she did come, I asked her for some.
She said, "No, dear." I said, "Your words aren't clear you'd better spit out your gum."
She screamed till her face got so red, then she fell on the floor,
And I covered her up and thought I'd go look through her drawer.

Verse 5:
And when I was through, I filled up my shoe and brought it to you.
And you, you took me in, you loved me then, you didn't waste time.
I, I never took much, I never asked for your crutch,
Now don't ask for mine.

79

Give A Little Bit

Words & Music by Rick Davies & Roger Hodgson

1. 3. Give a lit-tle bit,＿＿＿＿ give a lit-tle bit＿＿ of your love＿

＿ to me. I'll give a lit-tle bit,＿＿＿＿

I'll give a lit-tle bit＿＿ of my { love＿＿ to you. / life＿＿ for you.

There's so much that we need＿＿ to share,＿⌐ } so send a smile＿ and show＿
Now's the time＿ that we need＿＿ to share,＿⌐ }

＿ you care.＿ 2. I'll give a lit-tle bit,＿＿＿＿

I'll give a lit-tle bit＿＿ of my life＿＿ for you.

81

Golden Brown

Words & Music by
Jet Black, Jean-Jacques Burnel, Hugh Cornwell & David Greenfield

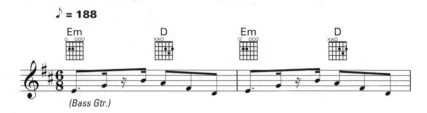

(Bass Gtr.)

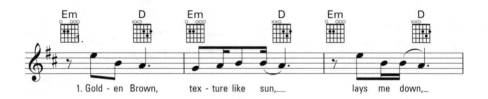

1. Gold - en Brown, tex - ture like sun,__ lays me down,__

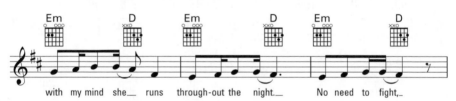

with my mind she__ runs through-out the night.__ No need to fight,__

1.

nev - er a frown__ with Gold - en Brown.__

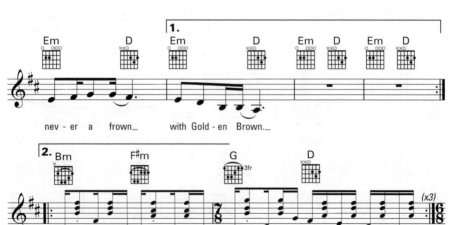

3. Gold - en Brown, fin - er temp - tress,

through the a - ges she's head-ing west, from far a - way,

stays for a day, nev - er a frown with Gold - en Brown.

Verse 2:
Every time is just like the last
On her ship, tied to the mast
To distant lands, takes both my hands
Never a frown with golden brown.

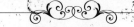

Get Off

Words & Music by Courtney Taylor-Taylor

Maybe you're gone,___ well if you find you find yourself against yourself.

Hey come on___ yeah, if you have a hard time gettin'there

To Coda ⊕

Maybe you're gone___ if you find you find yourself against yourself.

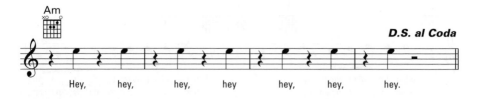
D.S. al Coda

Hey, hey, hey, hey hey, hey, hey.

⊕ Coda

Hey, hey, hey, hey, hey, hey, hey, hey,

hey, hey, hey, hey, hey, hey, hey.

The Gig Book
Jack Johnson

Good People

If the 1960s voice-and-guitar protest song was usually sung by someone who got their ideas from unreconstructed Socialism and their dress sense from singing hobo Woody Guthrie, today's songs with attitude can occasionally come from less radical performers. Ex-Hawaii surfer Jack Johnson began writing his laid back acoustic-type songs during his college years at the University of California Santa Barbara. His 2005 song 'Good People' may have a socially jaundiced lyric but musically it is as relaxed as Jackson himself is smooth.

Of the surfing accident that obliged him to change his leisure activities, Jackson jokingly like to claim that it was the 150-stitches head wound that made him so mellow. Perhaps, but with a strong track record in environmental activism Jackson just seems to be a different type of singer with a conscience.

Good People

Words & Music by Jack Johnson

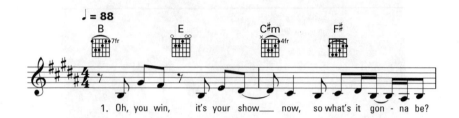

1. Oh, you win, it's your show___ now, so what's it gon - na be?

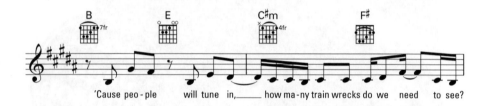

'Cause peo - ple will tune in,_____ how ma - ny train wrecks do we need to see?

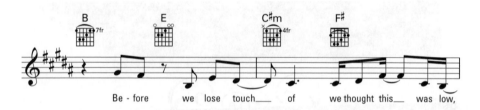

Be - fore we lose touch___ of we thought this___ was low,

___ oh, it's bad, get - ting worse___ so, where'd all the good peo - ple

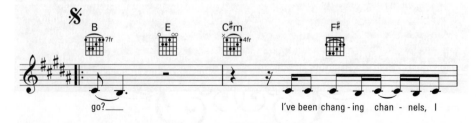

go?___ I've been chang - ing chan - nels, I

don't see them on the T. - V. shows._   Where'd all the good peo-ple go?__

To Coda | *1° only*

We got heaps and heaps of what__ we sow._   2. They got

this and that, with a rat-tle a tat,   test - ing__ one, two, now what ya gon-na do? Bad

news, mis- used, got too much to lose.   Gim-me some truth, now whose side are we on? What-

- ev - er you say,   turn on the boob tube,   I'm in the mood to o- bey.   So

lead me a - stray,   by the way__ now,   where'd all the good peo-ple

Sit-ting 'round, feel-ing far a - way.___

So far a-way___ but I can feel the de - bris. Can you feel___ it?

You in - ter - rupt me from a friend - ly con - ver - sa - tion,

to tell me how great it's all___gon-na be.___ You might no -

-tice some he - si - ta - tion. What's im-por-tant to you___ is not im-por-tant to me.

Oh, way down by the edge of your rea-sons,

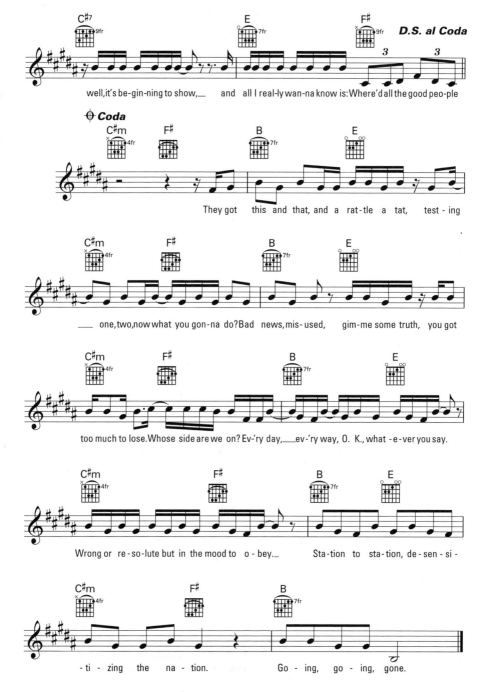

well, it's be-gin-ning to show,— and all I real-ly wan-na know is: Where'd all the good peo-ple

Coda

They got this and that, and a rat-tle a tat, test-ing

— one, two, now what you gon-na do? Bad news, mis-used, gim-me some truth, you got

too much to lose. Whose side are we on? Ev-'ry day,— ev-'ry way, O. K., what-e-ver you say.

Wrong or re-so-lute but in the mood to o-bey._ Sta-tion to sta-tion, de-sen-si-

-ti-zing the na-tion. Go-ing, go-ing, gone.

Half The World Away

Words & Music by Noel Gallagher

1. I would like to leave this ci - ty, this old town_ don't smell_ too pret-ty and

(Verse 2 see block lyrics)

I can feel the warn - ing signs run-ning a - round my mind._

And when I leave this is - land, I'll book my - self_ in-to a soul_ a - sy - lum,

'cause I can feel the warn - ing signs run-ninng a - round my_ mind._

So here I go_ I'm still scratch-ing a - round in the same_ old hole, my

bo - dy feels young but my mind___ is ve - ry old.___

So what do you say,___ you can't give me the dreams that are mine___ a - ny - way, you're

half___ the world a - way,___ half___ the world a - way,___

half___ the world a - way.___ I've been lost,___ I've been found but I don't

1.

___feel down.___ ___feel down.___ No I don't__

2.

___ feel down,__ no I don't___ feel down.

Repeat to fade

Don't feel___ down. Don't feel__

Verse 2:
And when I leave this planet, you know I'd stay but I just can't stand it
And I can feel the warning signs running around my mind
And if I could leave this spirit, I'd find me a hole and I'll live in it
And I can feel the warning signs running around my mind.
So here I go...

The Gig Book
Jeff Buckley

Hallelujah

This once obscure title from the Leonard Cohen songbook owes its belated fame to Jeff Buckley's 1994 studio recording and a TV talent show which made it an unlikely Christmas No. 1 in 2008. Dating from 1984 when Cohen's career was in the doldrums, 'Hallelujah' was always a great song although, it seems, one that came equipped with 80-odd potential verses due to what sounds like a severe bout of over-production in the Cohen song factory. The song is full of biblical references that include David, Bathsheba and King Saul as well as a nod to Samson and Delilah. Jeff Buckley's eclectic career was cut short by an ill-advised evening swim in a slackwater channel of the Mississippi River at Memphis, Tennessee. Contrary to rumour, his drowning was accidental and not drug-related, unlike the death of his father, Tim Buckley, a once well-known singer whom Jeff only ever met once. Meanwhile 'Hallelujah' lives on in innumerable cover versions including those by Rufus Wainwright, John Cale and Alexandra Burke.

Hallelujah

Words & Music by Leonard Cohen

Freely ♩ = 160

1. Well, I heard there was a se-cret chord that Da-vid played and it
(Verses 2-4 see block lyrics)

pleased the Lord, but you don't real-ly care for mu-sic, do ya?

Well, it goes like this: the fourth, the fifth, the mi-nor fall and the ma-jor lift, the

baf-fled king com-pos-ing Hal-le-lu-jah.___ Hal-le-

-lu-jah. Hal-le-lu-jah. Hal-le-lu-jah. Hal-le-

1-4.

-lu - - - jah. 2. Well, your

lu...   Hal - le - lu - jah.   Hal - le -

- lu - jah.___   Hal - le - lu - jah.   Hal - le - lu - jah.___

Verse 2:
Well, your faith was strong but you needed proof.
You saw her bathing on the roof,
Her beauty and the moonlight overthrew ya.
And she tied you to her kitchen chair
And she broke your throne and she cut your hair,
And from your lips she drew the Hallelujah.

Verse 3:
Well, baby, I've been here before,
I've seen this room, and I've walked this floor,
You know, I used to live alone before I knew you.
And I've seen your flag on the marble arch,
And love is not a victory march,
It's a cold and it's a broken Hallelujah.

Verse 4:
Well, there was a time when you let me know
What's really going on below,
But now you never show that to me, do ya?
But remember when I moved in you
And the holy dove was moving too,
And every breath we drew was Hallelujah?

Verse 5:
Maybe there's a God above,
But all I've ever learned from love
Was how to shoot somebody who outdrew ya
And it's not a cry that you hear at night,
It's not somebody who's seen the light
It's a cold and it's a broken Hallelujah.

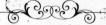

Hand In My Pocket

Words by Alanis Morissette
Music by Alanis Morissette & Glen Ballard

I'm   broke but I'm__ hap-py,__   I'm   poor but I'm kind,__   I'm
(Verses 2 & 4 see block lyrics, 3° Harmonica solo)

short but I'm__ health - y,   yeah.__   I'm__ high but I'm ground-ed,   I'm

sane but I'm ov-er-whelmed I'm   lost but I'm hope - ful, ba - by. And what it all comes down__

__ to   is that ev-'ry-thing's gon-na be   fine, fine, fine,_____

'cause I've_ got one hand in my pock-et   and the oth-er one is giv-in' a high five.

Verse 2:
I feel drunk but I'm sober
I'm young and I'm underpaid
I'm tired but I'm working, yeah
I care but I'm restless
I'm here but I'm really gone
I'm wrong and I'm sorry, baby
And what it all comes down to
Is that everything's gonna be quite alright
'Cause I've got one hand in my pocket
And the other one flickin' a cigarette.

Verse 3:
Harmonica solo
And what it all comes down to
Is that I haven't got it all figured out just yet
'Cause I've got one hand in my pocket
And the other one is givin' a peace sign.

Verse 4:
I'm free but I'm focused
I'm green but I'm wise
I'm hard but I'm friendly baby
I'm sad but I'm laughing
I'm brave but I'm chicken-shit
I'm sick but I'm pretty, baby
And what it all boils down to
Is that no one's really got it all figured out just yet
But I've got one hand in my pocket
And the other one is playin' a piano.

Happy Together

Words & Music by Alan Gordon & Garry Bonner

100

ba - by, the skies___ will be blue for all of my life.

5. Me and you___ and you and me, no mat-ter how they toss the dice,___ it has to

be. The on - ly one for me is you,___ and you for me, so hap-py to - geth - er.___

___ so hap-py to - geth - er.___ and how is the wea - ther?___

___ so hap-py to - geth - er.___ we're hap - py to - geth - er.___

___ so hap-py to - geth - er.___ so hap-py to - geth - er.___

___ so hap-py to - geth - er.___ so hap-py to - geth - er.

Verses 3+4:
Me and you and you and me
No matter how they toss the dice, it has to be.
The only one for me is you, and you for me,
So happy together.

Hey Ya!

Words & Music by André Benjamin

102

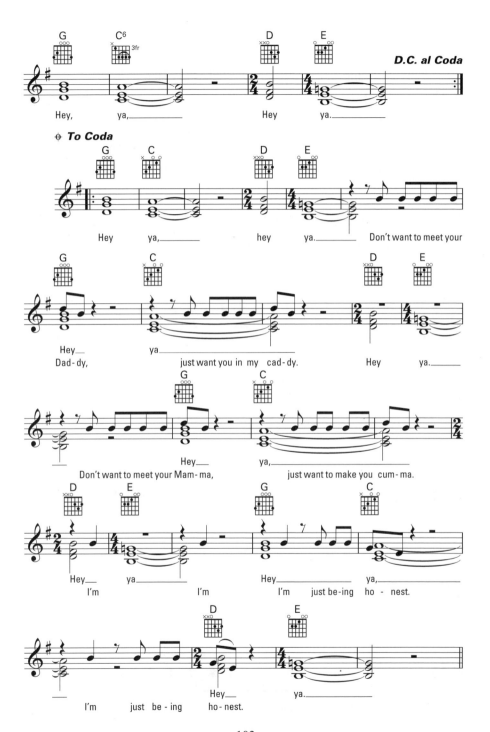

Hey, alright now alright now fellas (YEAH!) Now what's cooler than bein' cool? (ICE COLD!)
I can't hear ya', I say what's cooler that bein' cool? (ICE COLD!) whooo... Alright, alright, alright,
alright, alright, alright, alright, alright, alright, alright, alright, alright, alright, alright, ok now
ladies (YEAH!) and we gon' break this thing down for nothin' aow I wanna see y'all on y'all
baddest behaviour lend me some suga', I am your neighbour, ahh here we go!

Shake it   shake shake it   shake it   shake shake it   shake it   shake shake it   shake it

shake it   shake   shake it   shake it like a po - la - roid   pic - ture.   Hey ya.

Shake it   shake   shake it   shake it   shake   shake it   shake it

shake   it   shake   shake   it   shake   it   like   a   po - la - roid

pic - ture.   Shake it   shake shake it   shake it   shake shake it   shake it

Now Be-yon-cé's   and Lucy Lui's   And baby dolls, get on the floor

shake   shake   it   shake it like a po - la - roid   pic - ture.

You know what to   do.

104

Shake it shake shake it shake it shake shake it

shake it shake it shake shake it shake it like a po - la - roid.

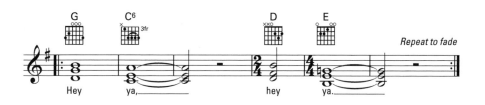

Hey ya,_____ hey ya._____

Verse 2:
You think you've got it, oh you think you've got it
But got it just don't get it till there's nothing at all
We've been together, oh we've been together
But seperate's always better when there's feelings involved
If what they say is (Nothing is for ever) then what makes
Then what makes, then what makes
Then makes, then, then what makes (love exception?)
So why you, why you, why you, why you, why you
Are we so in denial when we know we're not happy here.

105

How Deep Is Your Love

Words & Music by Barry Gibb, Maurice Gibb & Robin Gibb

♩ = 105

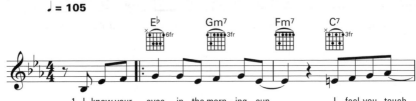

1. I know your eyes in the morn-ing sun.___ I feel you touch___
(Verse 2 see block lyrics)

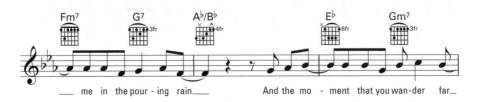

___ me in the pour-ing rain.___ And the mo-ment that you wan-der far___

___ from me, I wan-na feel you in my arms a-gain.___ And you come___

___ to me___ on a sum-mer breeze, keep me warm___ in your love, then you soft-

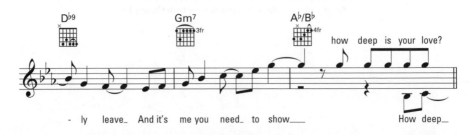

- ly leave. And it's me you need___ to show___ How deep___ how deep is your love?

106

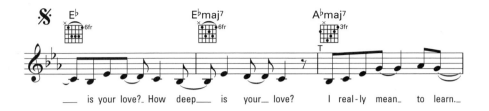

____ is your love?_ How deep____ is your_ love? I real-ly mean_ to learn.____

_____ 'Cause we're liv-ing in a world of fools,____ break-ing us

down, when they all____ should let us be,____ we be-long_

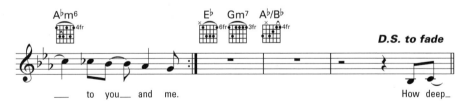

D.S. to fade

____ to you___ and me. How deep_

Verse 2:
I believe in you
You know the door to my very soul
You're the light in my deepest, darkest hour
You're my saviour when I fall
And you may not think I care for you
When you know down inside that I really do
And it's me you need to show
How deep is your love?

Hurt

Words & Music by Trent Reznor

1. I hurt my-self_ to-day to see if I_ still feel. I
(Verse 2 see block lyrics)
fo-cused on the pain,_ the on-ly thing that's real. The
nee-dle tears a hole,_ the old fa-mil-iar sting._ Try to
kill it all a-way_ but I re-mem-ber ev-'ry-thing._
What have I_ be-come_ my sweet-est friend?_

Verse 2:
I wear this crown of thorns upon my liar's chair.
Full of broken thoughts, I cannot repair.
Beneath the stains of time the feelings disappear.
You are someone else, I am still right here.

I Can't Make You Love Me

Words & Music by Mike Reid & Allen Shamblin

Verse 2:
I close my eyes, then I won't see the
Love you don't feel when you're holding me
Morning will come and I'll do what's right
Just give me till then to give up this fight.

I Don't Want To Wait

Words & Music by Paula Cole

ev - 'ry heart-beat sting - ing when she thought it was God— call-ing her.

Oh, would— her son— grow— to know— his fa -

- ther? I don't wan-na wait for our lives

— to be ov - er,— I want— to know— right now, what will it be?

I don't wan - na wait for our lives

1.

— to be ov - er,— will it— be yes— or will— it be— sor - ry?

— Do do do— do do do.— Do do do— do do do.— Do do do— do do do.

113

2.

C#sus4/G#   F#7

Oh,_____ so you look at me__ from a-cross

C#m7/G#

the room,__ you're wear-ing your an-guish a - gain.____ Be-lieve

Aadd9   Aadd9/E   B   Bsus4

__ me I know the feel-ing, it sucks___you in-to the jaws_ of an-ger.

F#7sus4

Oh._____ so breath a lit-tle more deep-ly in-to my

F#7   C#m7/G#

life, all we have is this ve-ry mo-ment.____ And

A

I don't wan-na do what his___ fa-ther and his fa-ther and

Aadd9/E   F#sus4   F#5   ***D.S. al Coda***

his fa-ther did. I wan-na be here now.____

So

114

Verse 2:
He showed up all wet on the rainy front step
Wearing shrapnel in his skin
And the war he saw lives inside him still
It's so hard to be gentle and warm
The years passed by and now he has granddaughters.

115

I Say A Little Prayer

Words by Hal David
Music by Burt Bacharach

1. The mo - ment I wake up, be-fore__ I put on__ my__
(Verse 2 see block lyrics)

make-up,__ I say a lit-tle prayer for you.__ While comb - ing my

hair now and won - d'ring what dress to__ wear now.__ I

say a lit-tle prayer for you.__ For - ev - er, and ev - er you'll stay in my heart and

I will love you for - ev - er and ev - er we nev - er will part,__ oh how I'll love you, to-

- geth - er, to-geth - er, that's how it must be.__ To live with - out you would

116

Verse 2:
I run for the bus dear
While riding I think of us dear
I say a little prayer for you
At work I just take time
And all through my coffee break time
I say a little prayer for you.

Hello Mary Lou

Words & Music by Cayet Mangiaracina & Gene Pitney

Hel - lo Ma - ry Lou, good-bye heart, sweet Ma - ry Lou I'm

so in love_with you._____ I knew, Ma - ry Lou, we'd nev - er

3° Fine

part, so hel - lo, Ma - ry Lou, good-bye heart._____ 1. You
2. I

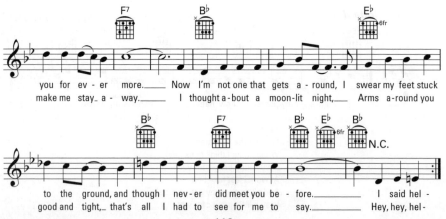

passed me by one sun - ny day,_ flashed those big brown eyes my way, and ooh, I want - ed
saw your lips I heard your voice, Be - lieve me I just had no choice, wild hors - es could - n't

you for ev - er more._____ Now I'm not one that gets a - round, I swear my feet stuck
make me stay_ a - way._____ I thought a - bout a moon - lit night,_ Arms a - round you

to the ground, and though I nev - er did meet you be - fore._____ I said hel -
good and tight,_ that's all I had to see for me to say._____ Hey, hey, hel -

118

Gordon Lightfoot

If You Could Read My Mind

Words & Music by Gordon Lightfoot

✦ Coda

feet. But sto‑ries al‑ways end, and if you read be‑

‑tween the lines, you'd know that I'm just tryin' to un‑der‑stand the

feel‑in's that you lack. I nev‑er thought_ I could

feel this way_ and I've got to say_ that I just don't get it. I don't know where

we went wrong, but the feel‑ing's gone_ and I just can't get it back._

molto rall.

Verse 2:
If I could read your mind, love
What a tale your thoughts could tell
Just like a paperback novel
The kind the drug‑stores sell
When you reached the part where the heartaches come
The hero would be me, but heroes often fail
And you won't read that book again
Because the ending's just too hard to take.

I'm With You

Words & Music by Avril Lavigne, Lauren Christy, Scott Spock & Graham Edwards

1. I'm stand-ing on the bridge, I'm wait-ing in the dark. I

(Verse 2 see block lyrics)

thought that you'd be here___ by now. There's

no-thing but the rain, no foot-steps on the ground. I'm

lis-ten-ing but there's___ no sound. Is-n't a-ny-one try'n to

find me? Won't some-bo-dy come take me home? It's a

damn cold night, try'n 'to fig-ure out this

123

124

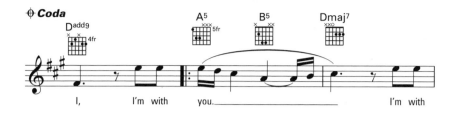

⊕ Coda

I, I'm with you._____ I'm with

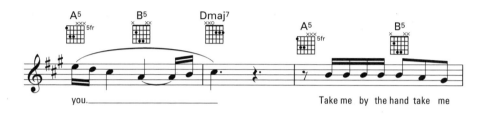

you._____ Take me by the hand take me

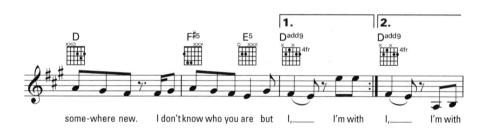

some-where new. I don't know who you are but I,____ I'm with I,____ I'm with

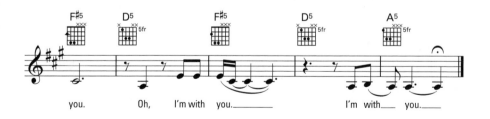

you. Oh, I'm with you._____ I'm with___ you.____

Verse 2:
I'm looking for a place, I'm searching for a face.
Is anybody here I know?
'Cause nothing's going right and everything's a mess.
And no one likes to be alone.

Imagine

Words & Music by John Lennon

Verse 3:
Imagine no possessions, I wonder if you can
No need for greed or hunger, a brotherhood of man
Imagine all the people sharing all the world
You may say I'm a dreamer, but I'm not the only one
I hope some day you'll join us, and the world will live as one.

Leave Right Now

Words & Music by Francis White

Mm._____ 1. I'm

(Verse 2 see block lyrics)
here just like I said though it's

break-ing ev - 'ry rule__ I've ev - er made.__ My rac - ing

heart is just the same why

make it strong__ to break it once__ a - gain.__

And I'd love to say__ I do,__ give ev - 'ry - thing__ to you,

how___ good it feels see-ing you to-day, and see you've got your smile_ back,

like_ you say you're right on track, but you may ne - ver know why

once_ bit-ten twice is shy,_ if I'm proud per-haps I should ex-plain

I could-n't bear to lose you a - gain.

Mm_____ mm_ mm mm._

Think I bet-ter leave right_ now be-fore I fall a - ny deep - er,

130

Verse 2:
I'm here so please explain
Why you're opening up a healing wound again
I'm a little more careful, perhaps it shows
But if I lose the high at least I'm spared the lows
Now I tremble in your arms, what could be the harm
To feel my spirit come.
So I say...

Linger

Words by Dolores O'Riordan
Music by Dolores O'Riordan & Noel Hogan

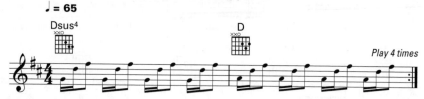

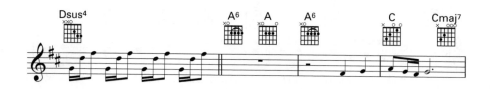

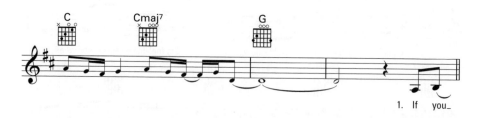

1. If you

if you could re-turn___ don't let it burn___ don't let it fade___

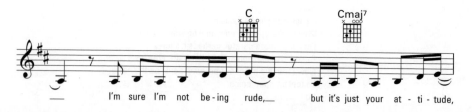

I'm sure I'm not be-ing rude,___ but it's just your at-ti-tude,

it's tear-ing me__ a-part,__ it's ru-in-ing ev-'ry-thing.__ 2. I swore,__

(Verse 3 see block lyrics)

I swore I would be true__ and ho-ney, so did you,__

so why__ were you hold-ing__ her

hand?_ Is that the way__ we stand?____ Were you ly-ing all__ the time?__

Was it just a game with you?__ But I'm in____ so

deep, you know I'm such a fool____ for you.

133

You got me wrapped a-round your fin-ger,___ ah,___ ah,___ ha.

Do you have to let it lin - ger? Do you have to, do you

1.

have to, do you have to let it lin - ger?___

Oh I thought the world of you,___ I thought no-thing could_ go wrong,

_____ but I was wrong,___ I was wrong,_____ 3. If you

2.

- ger?__

(Instr.)

Verse 3:
If you, if you could get by trying not to lie
Things wouldn't be so confused, and I would feel so used
But you always really knew I just wanna be with you.
But I'm so deep...

Joan Armatrading

Love And Affection

Words & Music by Joan Armatrading

I am not in love___ but I'm op - en

to per - sua - sion.__ East or West,___ where's the best___

for ro - manc - ing?___ With a friend

I can smile but with a lov - er I could hold my head_

___ back, I could real - ly laugh, real - ly laugh. Thank you,__

___ you took me danc - ing___ 'cross the floor,

137

Sing me an-oth-er love song but this time with a lit-tle de-di-ca-tion. Sing it,

sing it. (Sing it, sing it.) You know that's what I like. (Lov-er ooh ooh.)

Once more with the feel-ing. Oh, give me love,___ give___ me love, give me love.___

Love.

(Sax.)

Love Is All Around

Words & Music by Reg Presley

on my___ love___ you can de - pend.___

1.

Got to keep it mov - ing. It's

writ-ten in___the wind,___ oh,_____ ev-'ry-where I go.___ So

if you real-ly love me, come on and let it show._____ Come on and let it

Repeat to fade

show.)
Come on and let___ it, come on and let___ it, come on and let___ it___ show.

Verse 2:
I see your face before me as I lay on my bed
I kinda get to thinking of all the things you said
You gave your promise to me, and I gave mine to you
I need someone beside me, in everything I do.

Lovin' You

Words & Music by Minnie Riperton & Richard Rudolph

♩ = 62

Lov - in' you_____ is ea - sy 'cause you're beau - ti - ful, mak - in' love with you____ is all____ I wan - na do.__ Lov - in' you is more than just__ a dream come true, 'cause ev -'ry-thing that I do____ is out____ of lov - in' you.__ La la la la la la la la la la la la la la la la la la__ la la__ la, doo doo din doo doo,___ ah.___

144

No one else— can make— me feel— the co-lours that— you bring,—

stay with me— while we— grow old— and we—— will live each day in spring-time;

'cause lov - in' you———— has made my life———— so beau-ti-ful,
'cause lov - in' you———— is ea-sy 'cause——you're beau-ti-ful,

ev-'ry day of my life—— is filled——with lov - in' you.——

Lov - in' you,—— I see your soul— come shin-in' through,—

ev-'ry time that we oo——— I'm more in love— with you.——

D.S. al Coda

✧ Coda

Repeat to fade

La la la la la la la la la la la la la la la la la—— la la——la.

145

Maggie May

Words & Music by Rod Stewart & Martin Quittenton

Verse 2:
The morning sun, when it's in your face
Really shows your age
But that don't worry me none
In my eyes you're everything
I laugh at all your jokes
My love you didn't need to coax
Oh Maggie I couldn't have tried anymore
You led me away from home
Just to save you from being alone
You stole my soul and that's a pain I can do without.

Verse 3:
All I needed was a
Friend to lend a guiding hand
But you turned into a lover
And mother what a lover, you wore me out
All you did was wreck my bed
And in the morning kick me in the head
Oh Maggie I couldn't have tried anymore
You led me away from home
'Cause you didn't wanna be alone
You stole my heart I couldn't leave you if I tried.

Many Rivers To Cross

Words & Music by Jimmy Cliff

Ma-ny riv-ers to cross,___ but I can't seem to find___ my way over. Wan-der-ing, I am lost,___ as I tra - vel a-long___ ___ (the) white cliffs of Do - ver. Ma - ny rivers to cross,___ and it's on-ly my will that keeps me a - live. I've been licked, washed up for years.___ and I've_ mere-ly sur-vived_ be - cause of my pride._ But I, lone - li-ness won't leave me a-lone;

(Marie's The Name)
His Latest Flame

Words & Music by Doc Pomus & Mort Shuman

1. A ve-ry old friend came by to - day, 'cause he was
(Verse 2 see block lyrics)

tell - in' ev -'ry - one in town_ 'bout the love that he just found._

And Ma-rie's the name of his lat - est flame.

2. He talked and

Though I smiled, the tears in - side_ were a - burn-in'._____ I

wished him luck and then he said_ good - bye.

He was gone but still his words kept re - turn - in'._____ What
else was there for me to do__ but cry?
Would you be - lieve that yes - ter - day, this girl was
in my arms and swore to me__ she'd be mine e - ter - nal - ly?__ And Ma - rie's the

1.
name of his lat - est flame.

2.
flame. And Ma - rie's the name of his lat - est

Repeat to fade

Verse 2:
He talked and talked, and I heard him say
That she had the longest, blackest hair,
The prettiest green eyes anywhere.
And Marie's the name of his latest flame.

151

Missing

Words by Tracey Thorn
Music by Ben Watt

♩ = 128

1, 4. I step off the train, I'm walk-ing down your street
(Verse 2&3 see block lyrics)

a - gain, and past your door, but

you don't live there a - ny-more. It's years since you've been there,

and now you've dis-ap-peared some-where, like

out - er space you've found some bet-ter place. And I miss you

Verse 2:
And could you be dead?
You always were two steps ahead of everyone
We'd walk behind you while you would run
I look up at your house
And I can almost hear you shout down to me
Where I always used to be
And I miss you.

Verse 3:
Back on the train
I ask why did I come again?
Can I confess I've been hanging 'round your old address?
And the years have proved
To offer nothing since you've moved
You're long gone but I can't move on
And I miss you.

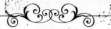

Maybe Tomorrow

Words & Music by Kelly Jones, Richard Jones & Stuart Cable

Ooh, bap_ a ooh,_ Ooh, bap_ a ooh,_ Ooh, bap_ a ooh,_

Ooh, bap_ a ooh,_ 1. I've been down and I'm won-de-ring why_ these

(Verse 2 see block lyrics)

lit - tle black clouds keep a - walk-ing a - round_ with me, with

me._ It wastes time and I'd rath-er be high_ I think I'll

walk me out - side and buy a rain-bow smile_ but be free,_ they're all_

free._ So may - be to-mor - row I'll find my

154

way_____ home.___ So may - be___ to - mor-

- row, I'll find my way_____ home.___ home.

Ah, ah, ah._____
Ooh, ooh,__ ooh, ooh,__ ooh, ooh,__ ooh, ooh.__

Ah, ah. ah,_____ ah._____
Ooh, ooh,__ ooh, ooh,__ ooh, ooh.__

Ooh, ooh, ooh, ooh.

So may - be to - mor - row I'll find my way_____ home._

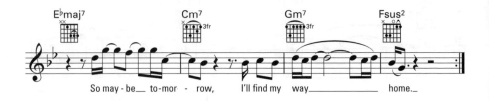

So may - be— to-mor - row, I'll find my way_____ home._

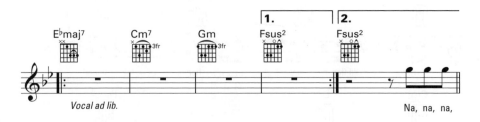

1. **2.**

Vocal ad lib.   Na, na, na,

na.   Na, na, na,   na.   Na, na, na,   na.   Na, na, na,   na.—   Na, na, na,

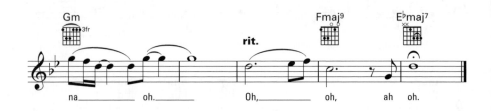

na_____ oh._____   Oh,_____ oh,   ah   oh.

Verse 2:
I look around at a beautiful life
I've been the upper side of down
Been the inside of out
But we breathe, we breathe
I wanna breeze and an open mind
I wanna swim in the ocean, wanna take my time
For me, all me.

More Than Words

Words & Music by Nuno Bettencourt & Gary Cherone

1. Say- ing, "I___ love___ you," is not the words I want___ to___ hear from you,___
(Verse 2 see block lyrics)

___ it's not that I___ want___ you, not to say,___ but if___ you___ on - ly knew___

___ how ea - sy___ it would be___ to show___ me how___ you feel.___

___ More than words___ is all you have___ to___ do___ to make it___ real.___

157

158

Verse 2:
Now that I've tried to talk to you and make you understand
All you have to do is close your eyes and just reach out your hand
And touch me, hold me close, don't ever let me go
More than words is all I ever needed you to show.

New York, New York

Words & Music by Ryan Adams

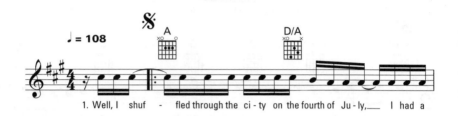

1. Well, I shuf - fled through the ci - ty on the fourth of Ju - ly,___ I had a

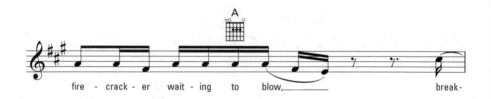

fire - crack - er wait - ing to blow,___ break-

- in' like a rock-et who was mak-ing its way_ to the ci - ties of Mex - i - co. Lived

___ in an a-part-ment out on A-ven-ue A,_ I had a tar hut on the cor-ner of tenth. Had_

___my-self a lo-ver who was fi-ner than gold, but I've been bro-ken up and bust-ed up since._

Love don't play any games with me anymore like she did before. The world won't wait so I better shake that thing right out there through the door. Well, I still love you New York.

2. Found

Hell, I still love you, New York.

New York.

3. I

161

Verse 2:
Found myself a picture that would stay in the folds of my wallet and it stayed pretty good
Still amazed I didn't lose it on the roof of the place when I was drunk and I was thinking of you
Every day the children, they were singing their tunes out on the streets and you could hear from inside
Used to take the subway up to Houston and third, I would wait for you and try to hide
Love won't play any games with you anymore if you don't want it to
The world won't wait and I watched you shake but honey I don't blame you
Hell, I still love you though, New York.

Verse 3:
I remember Christmas in the blistering cold in a church on the upper west side
Babe, I stood there singing, I was holding your arm, you were holding my trust like a child
Found a lot of trouble out on Avenue B but I tried to keep the overhead low
Farewell to the city and the love of my life, at least we left before we had to go
Love won't play any games with you anymore if you want them to
So we better shake this old thing out the door I'll always be thinking of you
I'll always love you though, New York.

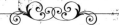

Nights In White Satin

Words & Music by Justin Hayward

1. Nights in white sa - tin,_____ nev-er reach-ing the end,
(Verse 2 see block lyrics)

let - ters I've writ - ten_____ nev-er mean-ing to send.

Beau-ty I'd al-ways missed, with these eyes be-fore, just what the truth is_____

I can't say an - y - more,_____ 'cause I love you,_____ yes, I_____ love you._____ Oh, how_ I

love_ you._____ how I_____ love you._____

Verse 2:
Gazing at people, some hand in hand
Just what I'm going through, they can't understand
Some try to tell me thoughts they cannot defend
Just what you want to be, you'll be in the end
And I love you, yes, I love you
Oh, how I love you, how I love you.

163

No Regrets

Words & Music by Tom Rush

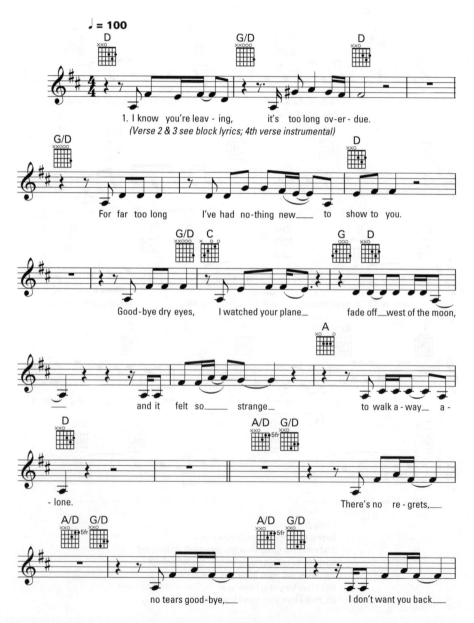

1. I know you're leav - ing, it's too long ov-er-due.

(Verse 2 & 3 see block lyrics; 4th verse instrumental)

For far too long I've had no-thing new____ to show to you.

Good-bye dry eyes, I watched your plane____ fade off____west of the moon,

____ and it felt so____ strange____ to walk a-way____ a-

- lone. There's no re-grets,

no tears good-bye,____ I don't want you back____

Verse 2:
The hours that were yours
Echo like empty rooms
The thoughts we used to share
I now keep alone
I woke last night and spoke to you
Not thinking you were gone
And it felt strange
To lie awake alone.
There's no regrets...

Verse 3:
Our friends have tried
To turn my nights to day
Strange faces, a new place
Can't keep the ghost away
Now just beyond the darkest hour
And just behind the dawn
It stills feels so strange
To lead my life alone.
There's no regrets...

Nothing Ever Happens

Words & Music by Justin Currie

1. Post of-fice clerks put up signs say-ing po - si - tion closed, and
2. "Gent - le - men time please you know we can't serve an - y - more". Now

(Verses 3 & 4 see block lyrics)

se - cre - t'ries turn off type - writ - ers and put on their coats. And
the traf - fic lights change to stop when there's noth-ing to go. And by

ja - ni - tors pad-lock the gates for se - cu - ri - ty guards to pa-
five o' - clock ev - 'ry-thing's dead, and ev - 'ry third car is a

-trol, and ba - che - lors phone up their friends for a drink, while the
cab, and ig - nor - ant peo - ple___ sleep in their beds like the

1.

mar - ried ones turn on a chat show. And they'll all be
doped white mice in the col - lege lab.

lone - ly to - night, and lone - ly to - mor - row.

166

And no-thing ev - er hap-pens, no-thing hap-pens at

all.

The nee-dle re-turns to the start of the song and we all sing a-
(last time) They'll burn down the sy-na-gogues at six o' - clock, and we'll all go a-

- long like be - fore. And we'll all be lone-ly to - night, and lone-ly to -
- long like be - fore.

Repeat chorus
then Fine

-mor-row.

D.C. al Fine

4. And

Verse 3:
The telephone exchanges click while there's nobody there
The Martians could land in the car park and no one could care
The close-circuit cameras in department stores shoot the same movie everyday
And the stars of these films neither die nor get killed just survive constant action replay.

Verse 4:
And bill hoardings advertise products that nobody needs
While 'Angry from Manchester' writes to complain about all the repeats on TV
And computer terminals report some gains in the values of copper and tin
While American businessmen snap up Van Goghs for the price of a hospital wing.

One Love/People Get Ready

Words & Music by Bob Marley & Curtis Mayfield

Let them all pass all_ their dir - ty re - marks. (One
Let's get to - geth - er_ to fight this Ho - ly Ar - ma - ged - don, (One

love.) There is one ques - tion I'd real - ly love to ask._ (One
love.) so when the Man comes there will be no, no doom._ (One

heart.) Is there a place for the hope-less sin - ner who has hurt all man-kind just to
song.) Have pi - ty on those whose chan - ces grow thin-ner. There ain't no hid-ing place from the

1.
save his own?_ Be - lieve me.

2.
D.S. al Coda
Fath - er of Cre - a - tion. Say - in',

⊕ **Coda**
thanks and praise to the Lord and I will feel all right."

Repeat to fade
Let's get to - geth - er and feel all right. "Give

169

One

Words & Music by U2

1. Is it get-ting bet-ter,___ or do you feel_ the same?_
(Verses 2 & 3 see block lyrics)

___ Will it make it ea - si-er on___ you,___ now___

you got___ some - one___ to blame?__ You___ say

one love,_ one life___ when it's one need___ in the night.

One love,_ we get_ to share it,___ leaves you ba - by if you

1, 2.

don't care_____ for it.___

170

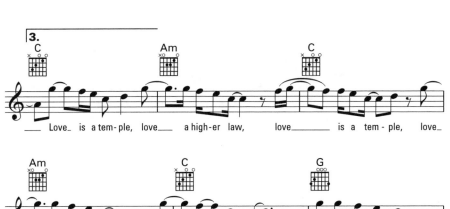

3.

— Love_ is a tem-ple, love___ a high-er law, love_____ is a tem - ple, love_

— the high-er law. You ask__ me_ to en-ter__ but then you make me crawl, and

I can't be hold-ing on_____ to what_you've got,_____ when all_you've got_ is hurt._

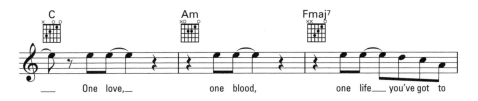

— One love,__ one blood, one life___ you've got to

do what you should. One life,__ with each oth - er:

sis - ters,_____ bro - thers.___ One life_____ but we're

171

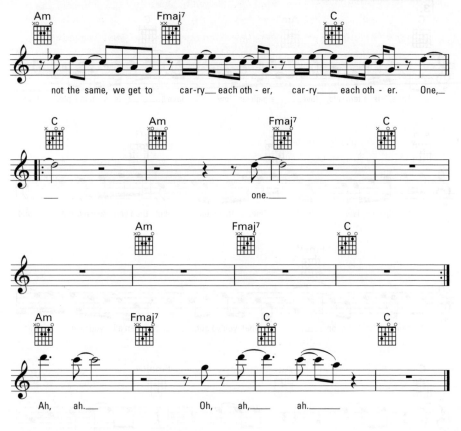

not the same, we get to car-ry__ each oth - er, car-ry___ each oth - er. One,__ one.___

Ah, ah.___ Oh, ah,___ ah._____

Verse 2:
Did I disappoint you
Or leave a bad taste in your mouth?
You act like you never had love
And you want me to go without
Well it's too late, tonight
To drag the past out into the light
We're one, but we're not the same
We get to carry each other, carry each other... one.

Verse 3:
Have you come here for forgiveness?
Have you come to raise the dead?
Have you come here to play Jesus
To the lepers in your head?
Did I ask too much, more than a lot?
You gave me nothing now it's all I got
We're one, but we're not the same
Well, we hurt each other, then we do it again. You say...

Other Side Of The World

There's nothing like an all-purpose song about longing and separation to appeal to a wide audience and KT Tunstall had her first solo hit in 2007 with 'Other Side Of The World'. After developing her style on the folk circuit, she had arrived fairly quickly and for many it was her performance at a 2005 London concert celebrating Bob Dylan's work that confirmed this Scottish singer/songwriter as the real deal. She closed a show full of venerable and worthy performers, but she was the new kid on the block and her passionate take on 'Tangled Up In Blue' identified her as a true Dylan fan even if she was born the same year as the song was first released. She has since recorded one overtly unplugged album (*KT Tunstall's Acoustic Extravaganza*), but at heart, Kate Victoria Tunstall was always an intensely personal one-woman-and-a-guitar kind of act, even when that guitar is complemented by a battery of foot-operated effects boxes or her backing group is in full swing.

Other Side Of The World

Words & Music by KT Tunstall & Martin Terefe

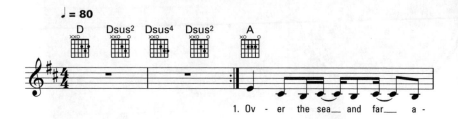

1. Ov - er the sea__ and far__ a-

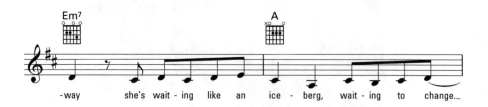

-way she's wait - ing like an ice - berg, wait - ing to change.__

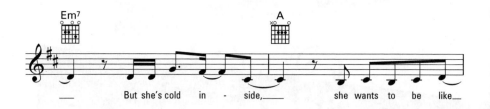

__ But she's cold in - side,__ she wants to be like__

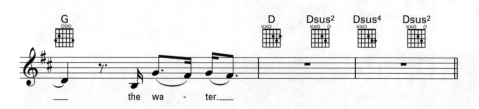

__ the wa - ter.__

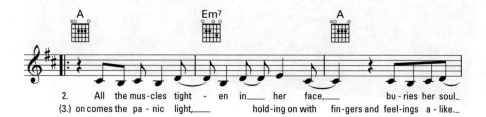

2. All the mus - cles tight - en in__ her face,__ bu - ries her soul__
(3.) on comes the pa - nic light,__ hold-ing on with fin-gers and feel-ings a - like.__

174

176

Pinball Wizard

Words & Music by Pete Townshend

he just does the rest.   He's got cra-zy flip-ping fin - gers,   nev-er seen him fall,   that

deaf, dumb and blind kid,   sure plays a mean pin - ball._____

Verse 2:
He stands like a statue
Becomes part of the machine
Feeling all the bumpers
Always playing clean
He plays by intuition
The digit counters fall
That deaf, dumb and blind kid
Sure plays a mean pinball.

Verse 3:
Ain't got no distractions
Can't hear no buzzers and bells
Don't see no lights a' flashin'
He plays by sense of smell
Always gets a replay
And never tilts at all
That deaf, dumb and blind kid
Sure plays a mean pinball.

I thought I was
The Bally table king
But I just handed
My pinball crown to him.

The Gig Book
Dire Straits

Romeo And Juliet

An achingly romantic song with a killer acoustic riff on a resonator guitar, 'Romeo And Juliet' was arguably Dire Straits' finest moment. If 'Sultans Of Swing' reflected the aspirations of an amateur band and 'Money For Nothing' bragged about the overblown rewards of rock stardom, 'Romeo And Juliet' was simply a great love song. Mark Knopfler's yearning, streetwise lyrics evoke both Shakespeare's famous balcony scene ('He's underneath the window') and *West Side Story*'s 'Somewhere' ('You know, the movie song'). In the end though it's the melody and that quietly insistent National Steel guitar figure that gave early notice of Knopfler's future shift away from stadium rock and towards Nashville where he would collaborate with everyone from Waylon Jennings and Chet Atkins to Emmylou Harris and John Fogerty.

Romeo And Juliet

Words & Music by Mark Knopfler

© Copyright 1980 Straitjacket Songs Limited.

1. A love-struck Ro-me-o sings a street-suss se - re - nade,_
(Verses 2 & 3, see block lyrics)

lay-ing ev-'ry-bo-dy low_ with a love song that_ he made,_

finds_ a street-light, steps out of the shade, says some-thing like,

"You and me babe,_ how a - bout it?"_

Ju - li - et says, "Hey, it's Ro-me-o, you near-ly gim-me a heart at- tack"

181

He's un-der-neath the win-dow, she's sing-ing "Hey la, my boy-friend's back,

you should-n't come a-round here, sing-ing up at peo-ple like that,"

An-y-way, what you gon-na do a-bout___ it?___ Ju-li-

- et, the dice were load-ed from___ the start,___ and I

(Chorus 2 & 3, see block lyrics)

bet, and you ex-plod-ed in-to my heart and I for-

- get, I___ for-get the mov-ie song.

182

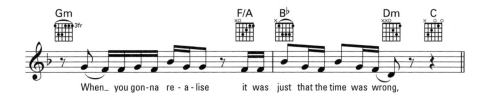

When_ you gon-na re - a - lise   it was just that the time was wrong,

(Play 3 times)

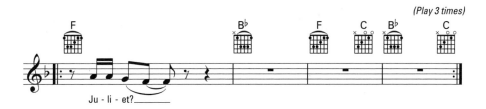

Ju - li - et?_____

Verse 2:
Come up on different streets
They both were streets of shame
Both dirty, both mean
Yes, and the dream was just the same
And I dreamed your dream for you
And now your dream is real
How can you look at me as if I was
Just another one of your deals?

Where you can fall for chains of silver
You can fall for chains of gold
You can fall for pretty strangers
And the promises they hold
You promised me everything
You promised me thick and thin, yeah
Now you just say "Oh Romeo, yeah,
You know I used to have a scene with him".

Chorus 2:
Juliet, when we made love you used to cry
You said, "I love you like the stars above,
I'll love you till I die."
There's a place for us, you know the movie song
When you gonna realise
It was just that the time was wrong, Juliet?

Verse 3:
I can't do the talks
Like they talk on the T.V.
And I can't do a love song
Like the way it's meant to be
I can't do everything
But I'd do anything for you
I can't do anything
Except be in love with you.

And all I do is miss you
And the way we used to be
All I do is keep the beat
And bad company
All I do is kiss you
Through the bars of a rhyme
Julie, I'd do the stars with you
Any time.

Chorus 3:
Juliet, when we made love you used to cry
You said, "I love you like the stars above,
I'll love you till I die."
There's a place for us, you know the movie song
When you gonna realise
It was just that the time was wrong, Juliet?

Shooting Star

Words & Music by Bob Dylan

Sing

Words & Music by Fran Healy

♩ = 136

Capo fret 2

1. Ba - by, you've been go - in' so cra - zy, late -
(Verse 2 see block lyrics)

- ly no - thin' seems to be go - in' right. So_

_ a - lone, oh, why d'ya have_ to get so_____ a - lone? You're_

_ sore you've been wait - in' in the sun too_____ long._____ But if you sing,

_ sing,_____ sing,_____ sing,_ sing,_

sing,_____ for the love you bring___ won't__ mean a thing

__ un-less you sing,___ sing,_ sing,_ sing._____

Ooh._____ Oh,_

__ oh,___ oh._____ Ooh._____

3. Ba - by, there's some-thing go - in' wrong to - day,__ but I say

no-thing, no-thing, no - thing, no-thing, no-thing, no-thing, no-thing, no-thing,

no - thing, no - thing. So____ na, na, na, na, now if___ you sing,_

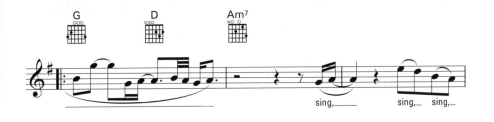

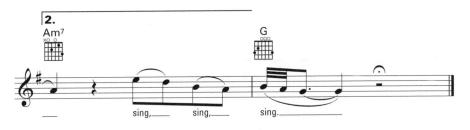

Verse 2:
Colder, crying over your shoulder
Hold her, tell her everything's gonna be fine
Surely you've been go-ing to hurry
Hurry, 'cause no one's gonna be stopped.
Not if you sing, sing...

(Sittin' On) The Dock Of The Bay

Words & Music by Otis Redding & Steve Cropper

190

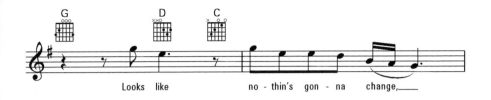

Looks like no - thin's gon - na change,____

ev - 'ry-thing still__ re-mains the same.   I can't do what

D.C. al Coda

ten peo-ple tell me__ to do,__   so I guess I'll re - main__ the same.__

⊕ Coda

Repeat ad lib. to fade

(Whistle)

Verse 2:
I left my home in Georgia,
Headed for the 'Frisco bay,
'Cause I've had no-thing to live for
And look like nothin's gonna come my way.
So, I'm sittin' on the dock...

Verse 3:
Sittin' here restin' my bones,
This loneliness won't leave me alone.
It's two thousand miles I roamed
Just to make this dock my home.
Now, I'm sittin' on the dock...

Solid Air

Words & Music by John Martyn

1. You've been tak-ing your time___ and you've been liv-ing on___ so - lid air.___

(Verses 3-6 see block lyrics)

You've been walk-ing the line___ and you've been liv - ing on___

so - lid___ air.___ Don't know what's go-ing wrong in - side,___

and I can tell you that it's hard to hide___ when you're liv - ing on___

so - lid___ air.___

2. And you've been paint-ing it blue___ and you've been look-ing through___ so - lid air.___

3.

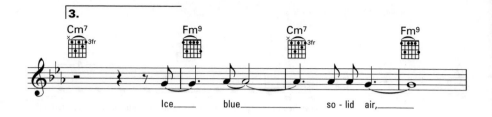

Ice___ blue_____ so - lid air,_____

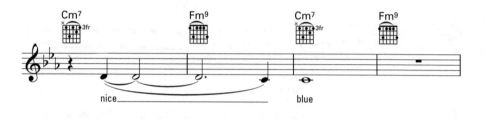

nice_____ blue

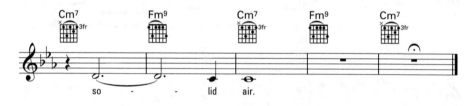

so - - lid air.

Verse 3:
You've been stoning it cold
You've been living on solid air
You've been finding it cold
And you've been living on solid air
I don't know what's going on inside
I can tell you that it's hard to hide
When you're living on solid air, solid air.

Verse 4:
You've been getting too deep
You've been living on solid air
You've been missing your sleep
And you've been moving through solid air
I don't know what's going on in your mind
But I know you don't like what you find
When you're moving through solid air, solid air.

I know you,...

Verse 5:
You've been walking your line
You've been walking on solid air
You've been taking your time
But you've been walking on solid air
Don't know what's going wrong inside
But I can tell you that it's hard to hide
When you're living on solid air, solid air.

Verse 6:
You've been painting it blue
You've been living on solid air
And you've been seeing it through
And you've been living on solid air
I don't know what's going on in your mind
But I can tell you don't like what you find
When you're living on solid air, solid air.

I know you,...

Something To Talk About

Words & Music by Damon Gough

196

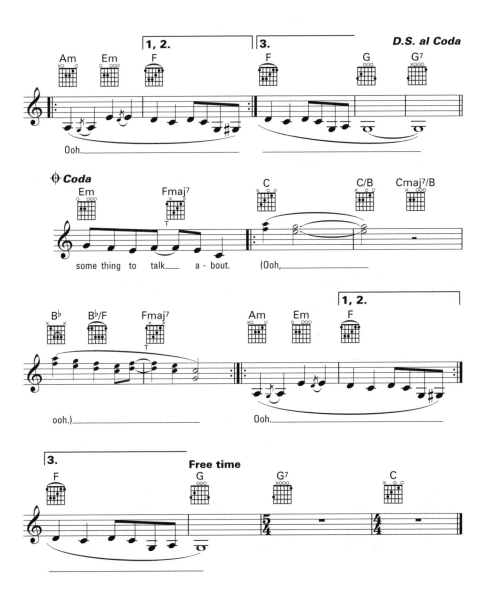

Verse 2:
Ipso facto using up your oxygen.
You know I'm, shallow, calling out for extra help.
You've got to let me in or let me out.

Verse 3:
I've been dreaming of the things I learned about a boy who's leaving.
Nothing else to chance again.
You've got to let me in or let me out.

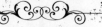

Songbird

Words & Music by Christine McVie

♩ = 77

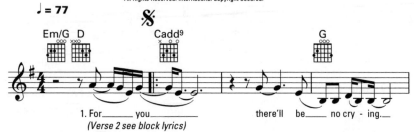

1. For_____ you_____ there'll be_____ no cry - ing._____
(Verse 2 see block lyrics)

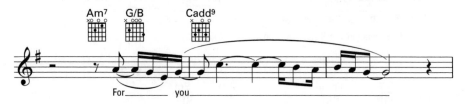

For_____ you_____

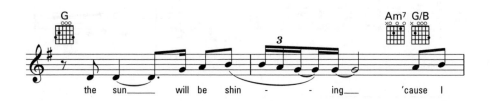

the sun_____ will be shin - - ing_____ 'cause I

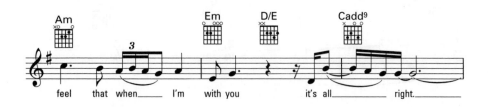

feel that when_____ I'm with you it's all_____ right._____

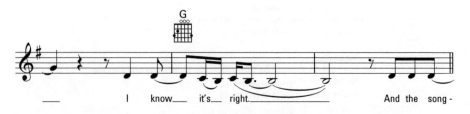

_____ I know_____ it's_____ right._____ And the song-

D   C   Em

- birds_____ keep sing-ing like they know__ the score._____

Bm/D   C

_____ And   I   love_____ you,   I   love_____ you,   I_____ love__

D⁷   To Coda ⊕ G   C   G   D.S. al Coda

you   like__ nev-er be-fore._____   2. To_____ you__

⊕ Coda

G   Am⁷ G/B C   G   Am⁷ G/B

be-fore._____   Like__ nev-er be - fore,_____

C   G

like   nev - er be - fore._____

Verse 2:
To you I would give the world
To you I'd never be cold
'Cause I feel that when I'm with you
It's all right
I know it's all right.
And the song birds...

199

Song To The Siren

Words & Music by Tim Buckley & Larry Beckett

1. Long a-float on ship-less o-ceans, I did all my best to smile,
(Verses 2 & 3 see block lyrics)
till your sing-ing eyes and fin-gers drew me, lov-ing, to your isle.
And you sang, "Sail to me,___ sail to me, let me en-fold you.

1.
Here I am, here I am,___ wait-ing to hold you."___

2.
sor - row.___

3.
hold___ you."___

Verse 2:
Did I dream you dreamed about me?
Were you here when I was fox?
But now my foolish boat is leaning
Broken, lovelorn, on your rocks
For you sing, "Touch me not,
Touch me not; come back tomorrow."
Oh my heart, oh my heart
Shies from the sorrow.

Verse 3:
Well, I'm as puzzled as the newborn child
I'm as riddled as the tide:
Should I stand amid the breakers
Or should I lie with Death, my bride?
Hear me sing: "Swim to me,
Swim to me, let me enfold you.
Here I am, here I am,
Waiting to hold you."

The Sound Of Silence

A simple song with a complex history, this Paul Simon composition perfectly caught the bleak post-Kennedy-assassination mood of America in 1964. It was originally recorded as an acoustic track for Simon & Garfunkel's debut album *Wednesday Morning, 3 A.M.* a record whose commercial failure led the duo to split up. However the track was later overdubbed with electric instruments by producer Tom Wilson and re-released as a single in September 1965. It was a hit. Sometimes titled 'The Sounds of Silence' (plural) it also appeared as a solo acoustic track—complete with foot-tapping—on *The Paul Simon Songbook* (1965). After this fitful start the song's success was finally assured and with it so was the career of Simon & Garfunkel who quickly reformed. They never looked back...at least not until the reunion tours some 40 years later.

The Sound Of Silence

Words & Music by Paul Simon

♩ = 113

Capo fret 1

1. Hel - lo dark - ness, my old friend,

I've come to talk to you a - gain, Be - cause a vi - sion soft - ly

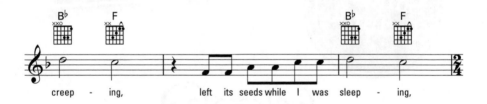

creep - ing, left its seeds while I was sleep - ing,

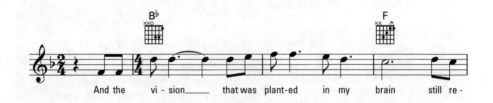

And the vi - sion_____ that was plant - ed in my brain still re -

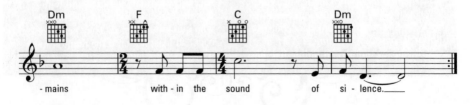

- mains with - in the sound of si - lence.____

Verse 2:
In restless dreams I walked alone
Narrow streets of cobblestone
'Neath the halo of a street lamp
I turned my collar to the cold and damp
When my eyes were stabbed the flash of neon light
That split the night and touched
The sound of silence.

Verse 3:
And in the naked light I saw
Ten thousand people, maybe more
People talking without speaking
People hearing without listening
People writing songs that voices never share
And no-one dare disturb
The sound of silence.

Verse 4:
"Fools!" said I, "You do not know,
Silence like a cancer grows.
Hear my words that I might teach you,
Take my arms that I might reach you."
But my words like silent raindrops fell
And echoed in the wells of silence.

Verse 5:
And the people bowed and prayed
To the neon god they made
And the sign flashed out its warning
In the words that it was forming.
And the signs said
"The words of the prophets are
Written on the subway walls and tenement halls."
And whispered in the sounds of silence.

Stay (I Missed You)

Words & Music by Lisa Loeb

Original key: Db (Tune guitar down a semitone)

♩ = 80

You say___ I on-ly hear what I want to.

You say___ I talk so all the time, so.___

And I thought what I felt was sim - ple, and I felt that I don't be - long,___

and now___ that I am___ leav - ing,___ now I know that I did some-thing wrong 'cause I

missed you.___ Yeah,_____ yeah, I missed you.___

And you say___ I on - ly hear what I want to: I

dy - ing since the day they were born, well. Well,

this is not____ that, I think that I'm throw - ing, but I'm

thrown.___ And I thought I'd live for - e - ver, but now I'm not so sure. You try to

tell me that I'm cle - ver, that won't take me an - y - how,___

___ or an - y - where___ with you.___

You said___ that I was na - ïve, and___ I thought that I was strong.___

I thought,___ "Hey, I can leave,___ I can leave." Oh,

206

Stuck In The Middle With You

Words & Music by Gerry Rafferty & Joe Egan

Capo fret 2

♩ = 124

1. Well I don't___ know why I came here to-night,___ I got the

(Verse 2, 3, 5 see block lyrics; 4° instrumental)

feel-ing that some thing ain't right.___ I'm so scared_ in case I fall off my chair,_

___ and I'm wond - 'ring how I'll get down the stairs.___ Clowns_

___ to the left___ of me, jok - ers to the right,___ here I am,_

___ stuck in the mid-dle with you.___ 2. Yes, I'm___ ___ Well, you

start-ted out with no-thing and you're proud that you're a self-made man.

208

And your friends they all come crawl - ing, slap__

__ you on your back and say "Please,_____

please."_____ 3. Well, I'm

5.

__ Yes, I'm__ stuck in the mid - dle with you.__

Stuck in the mid - dle with you.__

Verse 2:
Yes, I'm stuck in the middle with you
And I'm wond'ring what it is I should do
It's so hard to keep the smile from my face
Losing control, yeah, I'm all over the place.

Verse 3:
Well, I'm trying to make some sense of it all
But I can see it makes no sense at all
Is it cool to go to sleep on the floor?
'Cause I don't think that I can take anymore.

Verse 5:
Well, I don't know why I came here tonight
I got the feeling that something ain't right
I'm so scared in case I fall off my chair
And I'm wond'ring how I'll get down the stairs.

Sunday Morning

Words & Music by Lou Reed & John Cale

Original key: F (Tune guitar down one tone)

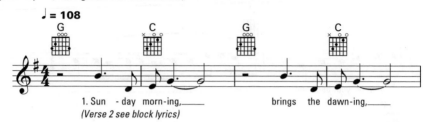

1. Sun - day morn-ing,_____ brings the dawn-ing,_____
(Verse 2 see block lyrics)

it's just a rest-less feel - ing by my side.___

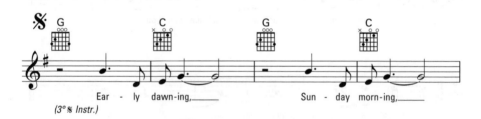

Ear - ly dawn-ing,_____ Sun - day morn-ing,_____
(3° % Instr.)

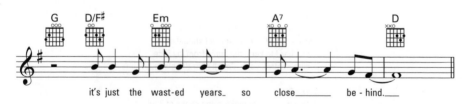

it's just the wast-ed years_ so close_____ be - hind.___

Watch out,___ the world's be-hind_____ you, there's al - ways some-

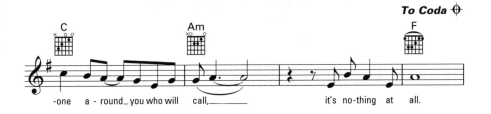

-one a - round_ you who will call,_____ it's no-thing at all.

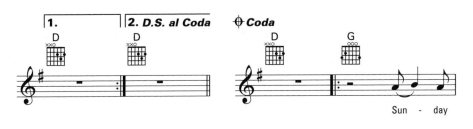

Sun - day

morn - ing. Sun - day morn - ing.

Verse 2:
Sunday morning and I'm falling
I've got a feeling I don't want to know
Early dawning, Sunday morning
It's all the streets you crossed, not so long ago.

Watch out,...

Sunshine Superman

Words & Music by Donovan Leitch

1. Sun-shine came soft - ly through my win-dow to - day,___

(Verses 2, 3 & 5 see block lyrics)
(Verse 4 instrumental)

could have tripped out ea - sy but I've changed my ways,___

it - 'll take time___ I know__ it but in a while,___

you're gon-na be mine___ I know it, we'll do it in style.___

'Cause I've made my mind up you're go - ing to be mine.___ I'll tell you right now,

213

Verse 2:
Superman and Green Lantern ain't got nothing on me
I can make like a turtle and dive for pearls in the sea
You can just sit there thinking on your velvet throne
I've followed the rainbow so you can have all your own.

'Cause I've made my mind up you're going to be mine
I'll tell you right now
Any trick in the book now baby that I can find.

Verse 3:
Everybody's hustling just to have a little scene
When I said we'd be cool I think that you know what I mean
We stood on a beach at sunset, do you remember when?
I know a beach where baby, it never ends.

When you've made your mind up forever to be mine.
Mmm... *(to 3° bar)*

Verse 4:
Instrumental

Verse 5:
Superman and Green Lantern ain't got nothing on me
I can make like a turtle and dive for pearls in the sea
You can just sit there thinking on your velvet throne
I've followed the rainbow so you can have all your own.

When you've made your mind up forever to be mine.
Mmm... *(to 5° bar)*

Space Oddity

Words & Music by David Bowie

♩ = 67

Ground con - trol___ to Ma - jor Tom,___

ground con - trol___ to Ma - jor Tom:___

Take your pro-tein pills and put your hel-met on.___   Ground con-trol_ to Ma - jor Tom:

Spoken: Ten,   *Nine,*

Com-men-cing count down: En - gines   on.

Eight,   *Seven,*   *Six,*   *Five,*   *Four,*   *Three,*

(Space craft lift-off effects)

Check ig - ni-tion and may God's love be with you.

Two,   *One,*   *Lift off!*

Fmaj7 Em7 A9 C9 D9 E9

Fine

(ad lib.)

C E7

Though I'm past one hun-dred thou-sand miles_____ I'm feel-ing ve-ry still._

F Fm C F

_____ And I think my space-ship knows which way to go,_____ tell my

Fm C F G E7b9

wife I love her ve-ry much, "She knows."_____ "Ground con-trol to Ma-jor Tom: Your

Am Am7 D7

cir-cuit's dead, there's some-thing wrong. Can you hear me Ma-jor Tom?_ Can you

C G

D.S. al Fine

hear me Ma-jor Tom?_ Can you hear me Ma-jor Tom?_ Can you"

Teardrop

Words & Music by Robert Del Naja, Grant Marshall, Andrew Vowles & Elizabeth Fraser

1. Love, love is a verb, love is a do - ing word.

Fear - less on my breath. Gen - tle im - pul - sion,

shakes, makes me light - er. Fear - less on my

breath. Tear - drop on the fi - re.

Fear - less on my breath.

2. The light of the day, black flow-ers blos - som. Fear - less on my

218

Suzanne

Songwriter/poet/performer Leonard Cohen's dreamy song about another man's wife was the high spot of his impressive first album, released in 1967. A skilful if understated acoustic guitar player, Cohen wrote, played and sang this haunting song about Suzanne Verdal, a free spirit who lived on the Montreal waterfront. It started life as a poem ('Suzanne Takes You Down') from Cohen's 1969 collection *Parasites of Heaven* and was first recorded by Judy Collins. For most people, though, it was Cohen's own version of 'Suzanne' that introduced them to the work of this Jewish Canadian poet who would go on to find cult fame as a highly original singer/songwriter. His preoccupation with the religious, the carnal and the darkly comic would inform more than 40 years of musical creativity and mixed commercial fortunes.

The Gig Book
Leonard Cohen

Suzanne

Words & Music by Leonard Cohen

1. Suz-anne___ takes you down___ to her___ place near the riv - er, you can
(Verses 2 & 3 see block lyrics)

hear the boats go by,___ you can spend the night be-side___ her. And you

know that she's half cra - zy, but that's___ why you want to be there. And she

feeds you tea and or - an-ges that come all___ the way from Chi - na. And just

when you mean to tell her that you have no love to give her, then she

gets you on her wave-length, and she lets the riv-er ans - wer that you've al-

- ways been her lov- er. And you want to tra-vel with her, and you want to tra-vel blind.___ And you know she will trust ___ you, for you've touched her per-fect bod - y with your mind.

1, 2.

3.

rit.

2. And mind.
3. Now Suz -

Verse 2:
And Jesus was a sailor
When he walked upon the water,
And he spent a long time watching
From his lonely wooden tower.
And when he knew for certain
Only drowning men could see him,
He said, "All men will be sailors then
Until the sea shall free them."
But he himself was broken,
Long before the sky would open.
Forsaken, almost human,
He sank beneath your wisdom like a stone.
And you want to travel with him,
And you want to travel blind,
And you think maybe you'll trust him,
For he's touched your perfect body
  with his mind.

Verse 3:
Now Suzanne takes your hand,
And she leads you to the river.
She is wearing rags and feathers
From Salvation Army counters.
And the sun pours down like honey
On our lady of the harbour.
And she shows you where to look
Among the garbage and the flowers.
There are heroes in the seaweed
There are children in the morning,
They are leaning out for love,
And they will lean that way forever.
While Suzanne holds the mirror.
And you want to travel with her,
And you want to travel blind,
And you know that you can trust her,
For she's touched your perfect body
  with her mind.

223

They Don't Know

Words & Music by Kirsty MacColl

1. You've been a-round for such a long time now, oh, may-be
(Verses 2 &3 see block lyrics)
I could leave__ you but I don't know how.__
And why should I be lone-ly ev-'ry night__ when I can
be with you?_ Oh yes, you make it right.._ And I don't__ lis-ten to the
guys who say__ that you're bad__ for me__ and I should turn you a-way.__ 'Cause

love.   No, I   don't___   lis-ten to their wast-ed   lines,__ got my eyes_

___ wide   op - en and I   see the   signs_   that they   don't_ know a - bout__

us   and they've nev - er heard   of___   love.

Verse 2:
I get a feeling when I look at you
Wherever you go now I wanna be there too
They say we're crazy but I just don't care
And if they keep on talking still they get nowhere
So I don't mind if they don't understand
When I look at you and you hold my hand.
'Cause they don't know about us...

Verse 3:
Baby there's no need for living in the past
Now I've found your love I'm gonna make it last
I tell the others not to bother me
'Cause when they look at you they don't see what I see
No I don't listen to their wasted lines
Got my eyes wide open and I see the signs.
That they don't know about us...

Tears In Heaven

Best known as the cathartic song that Eric Clapton co-wrote following the death of his child who accidentally fell from the window of a 53rd floor apartment in Manhattan, 'Tears In Heaven' first appeared in the 1991 movie *Rush*. This uncompromising drug-bust movie already contained one song commissioned from Clapton and Texan lyricist Will Jennings who, with some reluctance, agreed to help Clapton complete 'Tears In Heaven' even though he felt such a personal song should be Clapton's alone. With its high vocal and acoustic guitar intro, 'Tears In Heaven' stands in marked contrast to much of Clapton's blues-driven work and electric guitar-hero image. It joined 'Help Me Up' in *Rush* and then became a hit. It has since been much covered although Clapton himself decided to stop playing it in 2004.

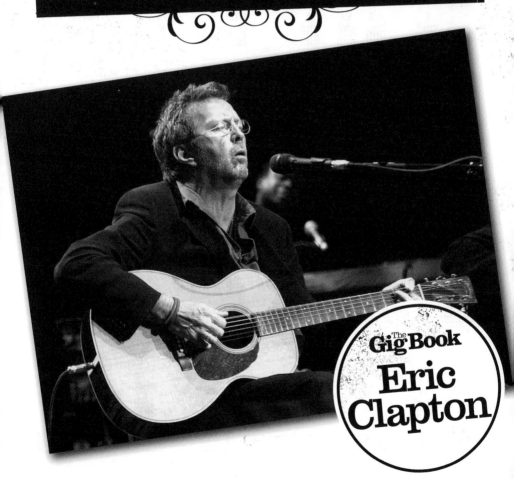

The Gig Book

Eric Clapton

227

Tears In Heaven

Words & Music by Eric Clapton & Will Jennings

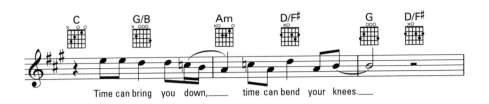

Time can bring you down,_____ time can bend your knees._____

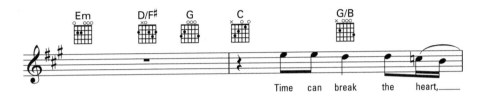

Time can break the heart,_____

D.C. al Coda

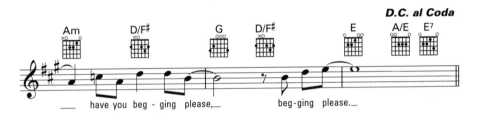

_____ have you beg - ging please,_ beg-ging please._

Coda

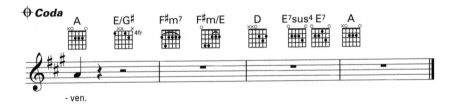

- ven.

Verse 2:
Would you hold my hand if I saw you in heaven?
Would you help me stand if I saw you in heaven?
I'll find my way through night and day
'Cause I know I just can't stay here in heaven.

Verse 3:
Instrumental solo for first 8 bars

Beyond the door there's peace, I'm sure
And I know there'll be no more tears in heaven.

229

That's Entertainment

Words & Music by Paul Weller

Capo fret 3

1. A po-lice car and a scream-ing sir - en, pneu-mat-ic drill and ripped_
(Verses 2-6 see block lyrics)

_ up con - crete. A ba-by wail-ing, stray_ dog howl-ing,

a screech of brakes, a lamp_ light blink - ing. That's en - ter-

1, 5.

To Coda

-tain - ment, that's en - ter - tain - ment.

D.S. al Coda I

2, 3.

Aah, la, la, la, la, la, ah,_ la, la, la, la, la.

Coda I

Aah, la la la la la ah,_ la la la la la. ah,_

230

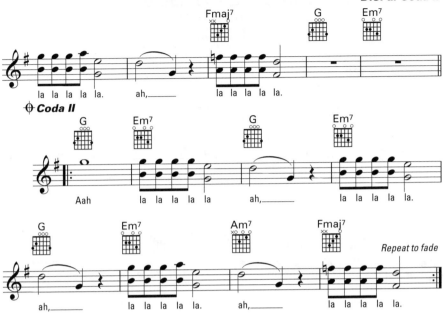

Coda II

Verse 2:
A smash of glass and the rumble of boots
An electric train and a ripped up phone booth
Paint splattered walls and the cry of a tom-cat
Lights going out and a kick in the balls, I say:

Verse 3:
Days of speed and slow time Mondays
Pissing down with rain on a boring Wednesday
Watching the news and not eating your tea
A freezing cold flat and damp on the walls.

Verse 4:
Waking up at 6 a.m. on a cool warm morning
Opening the windows and breathing in petrol
An amateur band rehearsing in a nearby yard
Watching the telly and thinking about your holidays.

Verse 5:
Waking up from bad dreams and smoking cigarettes
Cuddling a warm girl and smelling stale perfume
A hot summers' day and sticky black tarmac
Feeding ducks in the park and wishing you were faraway.

Verse 6:
Two lovers kissing amongst the scream of midnight
Two lovers missing the tranquility of solitude
Getting a cab and travelling on buses
Reading the grafitti about slashed seat affairs.

There She Goes

Words & Music by Lee Mavers

1. There she goes,___ there she goes_ a - gain,___
(Verses 2 & 4 see block lyrics)

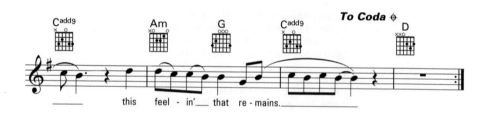

rac - ing through my___ brain.___ And I___ just___ can't con - tain___

___ this feel - in'___ that re - mains.___

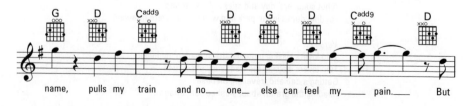

3. There she goes,___ there she goes_ a - gain.___ She calls my

name, pulls my train and no___ one___ else can feel my___ pain.___ But

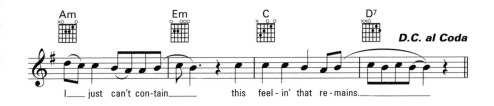

I__ just can't con-tain_____ this feel-in' that re-mains._____

⊕ Coda

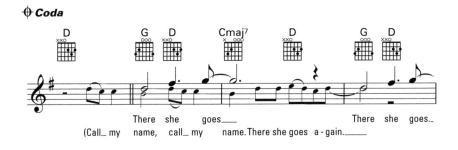

There she goes____ There she goes._
(Call_ my name, call_ my name. There she goes a - gain._____

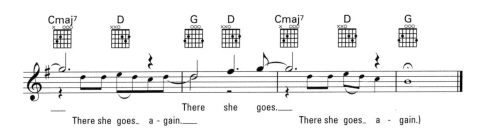

There she goes.____
There she goes_ a - gain.____ There she goes_ a - gain.)

Verse 2:
There she blows
There she blows again
Pulsing through my vein
And I just can't contain
This feelin' that remains.

Verse 4:
There she goes
There she goes again
Chasing down my lane
And I just can't contain
This feelin' that remains.

233

Torn

Words & Music by Anne Preven, Phil Thornalley & Scott Cutler

1. I thought I saw a man brought to life, he was warm, he came a-round like he was dig - ni-fied, he showed me what it was to cry.

Well, you could-n't be that man I a-dored,
(Verse 2 see block lyrics)
you don't seem to know, don't seem to care what your heart is for but I don't know him a-ny-more, there's

no-thing where he used to lie, my con-ver-sa-tion has run dry, that's what's go-ing on
(Verse 3 see block lyrics)
Chorus

no - thing's fine, I'm torn. I'm all out of faith, this is how I

Dm   **B♭**   **F**

feel, I'm cold and I___am shamed___ ly - ing na - ked on the floor.___ } Il - lu-sion nev - er changed
4° I'm cold and I'm_ a - shamed_ bound and bro - ken on the floor.___ }

C   **Dm**   **B♭**

___ in - to some-thing real,___ wide a-wake and I___ can see_the per - fect sky_ is torn,

F   **C**   **Dm**   **B♭maj⁷**

___ you're a lit - tle late___ I'm___ al - rea - dy torn.___

D.S. repeat Chorus
ad lib. to fade

Dm **Dm/C** **B♭**   **Dm**   **F**   **C**

Torn.___   Ooh___ ooh ooh.___ There's

Verse 2:
So I guess the fortune-teller's right
I should have seen just what was there
And not some holy light
But you crawled beneath my veins
And now I don't care I had no luck
I don't miss it all that much
There's just so many things
That I can't touch, I'm torn.

Verse 3:
There's nothing where he used to lie
My inspiration has all run dry
That's what's going on
Nothing's right, I'm torn.

Train In Vain

Words & Music by Mick Jones & Joe Strummer

1. You say_ you stand_ by__ your man, tell me some-
(Verses 2 & 3 see block lyrics)

-thing I don't un-der-stand.__ You said you

love me and there's a fact____ and then you left me, said you felt

trapped. Well some things you can ex-plain_ a-way,__ but the

heart-ache's in me till this day.__ You did-n't stand by

To Coda ⊕

me? No, not at all,_____ you did-n't stand by me. No

236

237

Verse 2:
All the times when we were close
I remember these things the most
I see all my dreams come tumbling down
I can't be happy without you around
So alone I keep the wolves at bay
And there's only one thing I can say.
You didn't stand...

Verse 3:
Now I got a job but it don't pay
I need new clothes, I need somewhere to stay
But without all of these things I can do
Without your love I won't make it through
But you don't understand my point of view
I suppose there's nothing I can do.
You didn't stand...

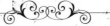

Vincent

Words & Music by Don McLean

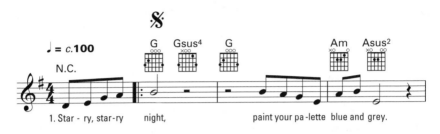

1. Star - ry, star - ry night, paint your pa - lette blue and grey.

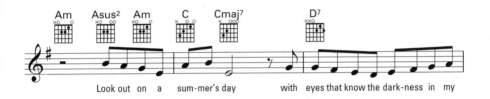

Look out on a sum - mer's day with eyes that know the dark - ness in my

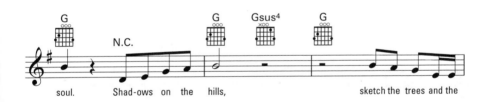

soul. Shad - ows on the hills, sketch the trees and the

daf - fo - dils. Catch the breeze and the win - ter chills, in

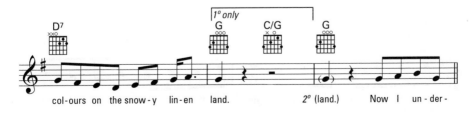

col - ours on the snow - y lin - en land. 2º (land.) Now I un - der-

do.   But I   could have told you Vin- cent,   this world was nev-er meant for one as

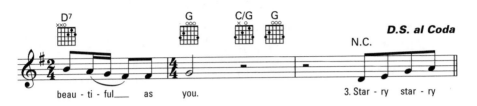

N.C.   **D.S. al Coda**

beau - ti - ful___   as   you.   3. Star - ry   star - ry

Coda

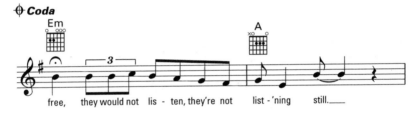

free,   they would not lis - ten, they're not   list -'ning   still.___

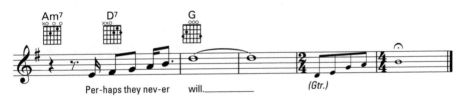

Per-haps they nev-er   will._____   *(Gtr.)*

Verse 3:
Starry starry night
Portraits hung in empty halls
Frameless heads on nameless wall
With eyes that watch the world and can't forget
Like the strangers that you've met
The ragged men in ragged clothes
A silver thorn of bloody rose
Lie crushed and broken on the virgin snow.

Now I think I know
What you tried to say to me
And how you suffered for your sanity
And how you tried to set them free
They would not listen
They're not list'ning still
Perhaps they never will.

Walk Right In

Words & Music by Gus Cannon & H.Woods

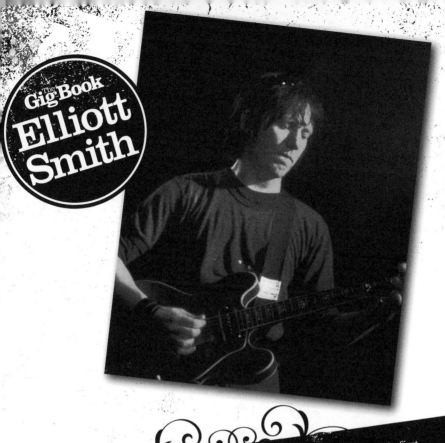

Waltz #2 (XO)

It may be tempting to see Elliott Smith as the sort of misfit whose personal pain was transfigured and redeemed by his musical art, but the man himself, who died at 34 a probable suicide, would have had none of it. He wrote intensely personal lyrics that never romanticized his demons—alcoholism, drug addiction and depression.

'Waltz #2 (XO)' came from his first album for DreamWorks Records, titled *XO* (the symbols for a kiss and a hug). This impressionistic song references Don & Phil Everly's 'Cathy's Clown' and Betty Everett's 'You're No Good'; to Smith aficionados clued-up on his upbringing, it would seem to be about the singer's bleak childhood. But for his thin voice Smith might have been the archetypal lone singer-songwriter strumming an acoustic guitar and singing. Instead he tended to multi-track his voice and instrumentation to create layers, textures, and harmonies that contrast oddly with his unadorned, stripped-down lyrics.

Waltz #2 (XO)

Words & Music by Elliott Smith

Original key: G minor (Tune guitar down one tone)

1. First the mic,___ then a half___ ci-gar-ette,___

(Verses 2 & 3 see block lyrics)

sing-ing "Ca-thy's Clown":_____ that's the man ___ she's mar-ried to now,___ that's the girl___ that he takes___ a-round town.___ She ap-pears___ com-posed,___ so she is,___ I sup-pose,___ who can real-ly tell?_____ She shows

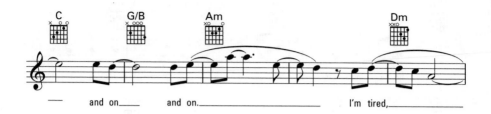

and on___ and on._____ I'm tired,_____

D.C. al Coda

— I'm tired._____

Coda

— I'm nev-er gon - na know___ you now,___ but I'm_
(Vocal tacet 3°)

— gon-na love you a - ny - how.___

Verse 2:
Now she's done and they're calling someone
Such a familiar name
I'm so glad that my memory's remote
'Cause I'm doing just fine
Hour to hour, note to note
Here it is, the revenge to the tune
"You're no good, you're no good,
you're no good, you're no good."
Can't you tell that it's well understood?

Verse 3:
Looking out on the substitute scene
Still going strong!
And it's, X O, mom
It's okay it's alright
Nothing's wrong
Tell mister man with impossible plans
To just leave me alone
In the place where I make no mistakes
In the place where I have what it takes.

Weather With You

Words & Music by Neil Finn & Tim Finn

1. Walk-ing round the room sing-ing "Storm - y Wea - ther" at fif-ty

se - ven Mount Pleas-ant Street___ Well, it's the same room but ev - 'ry-thing's diff-

- 'rent, you can fight the sleep but not the dream.___ Things ain't cook-ing

in my kit-chen strange af-flic - tion wash ov - er___ me.

Ju - li - us Cae - sar and the Ro - man Em - pire

could-n't con - quer the blue_____ sky_____

(Instr.)

Ev -'ry-where you go_

_____ you al - ways take the wea - ther with you_ ev -'ry-where you go_

_____ you al - ways take the wea - ther_ Ev -'ry-where you go_

_____ you al - ways take the wea - ther with you___ Ev -'ry where you go_

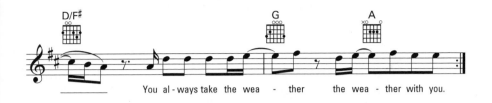

You al - ways take the wea - ther the wea - ther with you.

(Instr.)

D.S. al Coda

Ev - 'ry - where you go___

✠ Coda

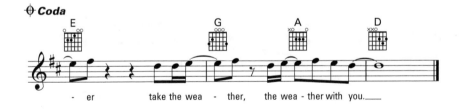

- er take the wea - ther, the wea - ther with you.___

Verse 2:
Well, there's a small boat made of china
It's going nowhere on the mantelpiece
Well, do I lie like a lounge-room lizard
Or do I sing like a bird released?

The Weight

Words & Music by Robbie Robertson (The Band)

1. I pulled in-to Na-za-reth, was feel-in' 'bout half-past dead.
(Verses 2-5 see block lyrics)

I just need some place where I can lay my head.

"Hey, mis-ter can you tell me where a man might find a bed?"

He just grinned and shook my hand, "No." was all he said.

Take a load off Fan-ny, take a load for free.

Take a load off Fan-ny, and and you

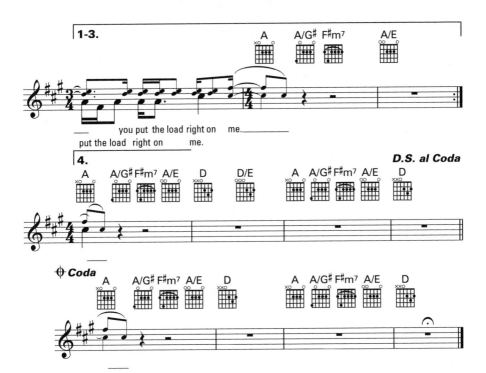

Verse 2:
I picked up my bag, I went looking for a place to hide
When I saw Carmen and the devil walking side by side
I said "Hey, Carmen, come on, let's go down-town."
She said, "I gotta go, but my friend can stick around."
Take a load off, Fanny...

Verse 3:
Go down, Miss Moses, there's nothing you can say
It's just ol' Luke, and Luke's waiting on the judgement day
"Well, Luke, my friend, what about young Anna Lee?" He said,
"Do me a favour son, won't you stay and keep Anna Lee company?"
Take a load off, Fanny...

Verse 4:
Crazy Chester followed me and he caught me in the fog
He said, "I will fix your rack if you take Jack, my dog."
I said, "Wait a minute, Chester, you know, I'm a peaceful man."
He said, "That's okay boy, won't you feed him when you can?"
Take a load off, Fanny...

Verse 5:
Catch a cannonball, now, to take me down the line
My bag is sinking low and I do believe it's time
To get back to Miss Fanny, you know, she's the only one
Who sent me here with her regards for everyone.
Take a load off, Fanny ...

251

What A Wonderful World

Words & Music by George Weiss & Bob Thiele

1. I see trees of green,___ red___ ro-ses too. I see them bloom,___ for me and you,___ and I think to my-self, what a won-der-ful world.___ 2. I see skies of blue,___ and clouds of white. The bright bless-ed day, the dark sa-cred night,___ and I think to my-self,___ what a won-der-ful world.___ The

colours of the rain-bow,__ so pret-ty__ in the sky,__ are
al-so on the fa-ces of peo-ple go-ing by. I see friends sha-king hands say-ing
"How do you do?"__ They're real-ly say-ing:__ "I love you." 3. I hear
ba-bies cry, I watch them grow, they'll learn much more
than I'll__ ev-er know. And I think to my-self what a won-der-ful world.
Yes,_____ I think to my-self,__
what a won-der-ful__ world. Oh, yeah.

When You're Gone

Words & Music by Bryan Adams & Eliot Kennedy

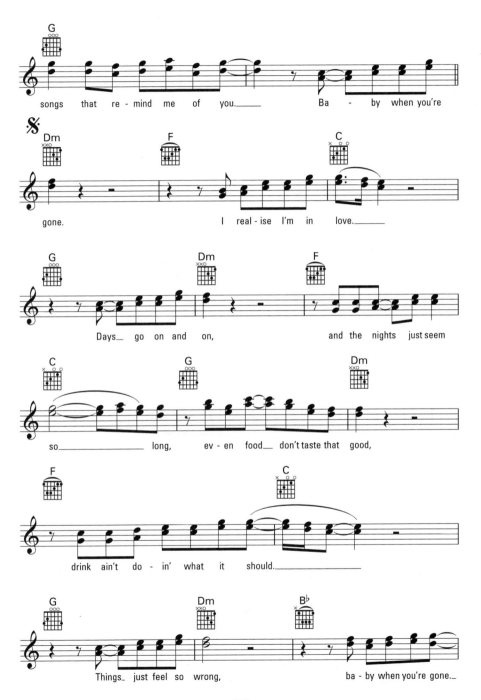

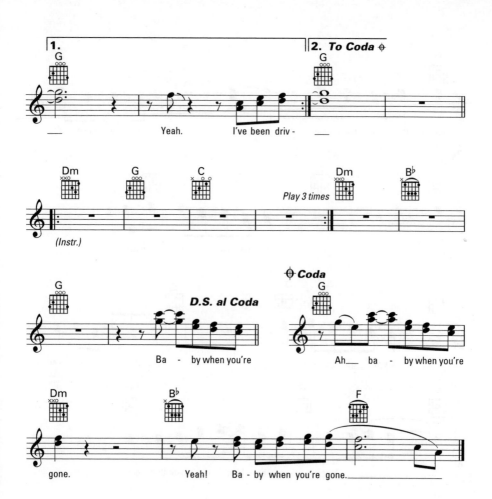

Verse 2:
I've been drivin' up and down these streets
Tryin' to find somewhere to go
Yeah I'm looking for a familiar face
But there's no one I know
Ah, this is torture this is pain
It feels like I'm gonna go insane
I hope you're comin' back real soon
'Cause I don't know what to do.

Will You

Words by Hazel O'Connor
Music by Wesley Magoogan & Hazel O'Connor

1. You drink your cof-fee and
(On D.S. sax solo)

I sip my tea, and we're sit-ting here play-ing so cool,_ think-ing

"What will be will be?" Oh, it's get-ting kind of

late now, oh, I won-der if you'll stay now, stay now,

stay now, stay now. Or will you_ just po-lite - ly say good

1.
- night? (Sax.)

2, 3.
- night?

257

Verse 2:
I move a little closer to you
Not knowing quite what to do
And I'm feeling all fingers and thumbs
I spill my tea, oh, silly me.

259

Who'll Stop The Rain

Words & Music by John Fogerty

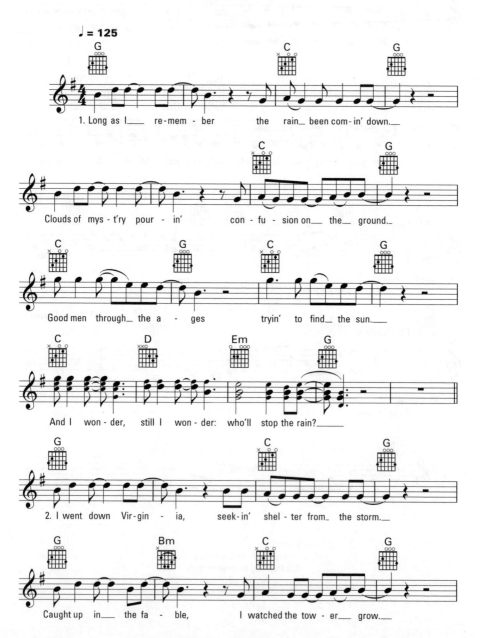

Five year plans__ and new__deals, wrapped in gol - den chains.__

And I won - der, still I won - der: who'll stop the rain?_____

3. Heard the sing - ers play - in', how__ we cheered for more.__ The

crowd had rushed to - geth - er, try - ing to____ keep__ warm.__

Still the rain__kept pour - in',__ fall - ing on__ my__ ears.__

And I won - der, still I won - der: who'll stop the rain?_____

Wild Wood

Words & Music by Paul Weller

1. High tide,___ mid-af-ter-noon, peo-
(Verses 2-5 see block lyrics)
- ple fly by in the traf-fic's boom.___
Know - ing___ just where you're blow - ing___ get-
- ting to where___ you___ should be go - ing.___

1. **2.4.** **5.**
And I say

climb - ing, for ev - er___ try - ing, you're gon-na

find your way out   of the wild, wild wood.

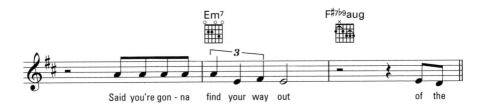

Said you're gon - na find your way out   of the

wild, wild__ wood.__   Of the

Verse 2:
Don't let them get you down
Making you feel guilty about...
Golden rain will bring you riches
All the good things you deserve now.

Verse 3:
Climbing, forever trying
Find your way out of the wild wild wood
Now there's no justice
You've only yourself that you can trust in.

Verse 4:
And I said high tide, mid-afternoon
People fly by in the traffic's boom
Knowing just where you're blowing
Getting to where you should be going.

Verse 5:
Day by day your world fades away
Waiting to feel all the dreams that say
Golden rain will bring you riches
All the good things you deserve now.

Yellow

Words & Music by Guy Berryman, Chris Martin, Jon Buckland & Will Champion

♩ = 88

1. Look at the stars, look how they shine for_____ you,
(Verse 2 see block lyrics)

and ev-'ry-thing you_ do.____ And they were all___ yel - low.___

I came a-long, I wrote a song for_____ you, and all the things you_ do,

___ and it was called yel-low.____ So then I took my____

___ turn.____ Oh, what a thing to have done.____

And it was all____ yel - low._____

Verse 2:
I swam across, I jumped across for you
Oh, what a thing to do, 'cause you were all yellow
I drew a line, I drew a line for you
Oh what a thing to do, and it was all yellow.

The Winner Takes It All

Words & Music by Benny Andersson & Björn Ulvaeus

all, the los-er stand-ing small be-side the vic-to-

-ry,_____ that's__ her des-ti - ny._____ 2. I was in your

2, 3.

The win-ner takes it all, the los-er has to

fall. It's sim - ple and it's__ plain,_ why should I

com- plain? **1.** 3. But tell me,_ ___ **2.** *D.S. al Coda* 4. I don't wan-na

✦ *Coda*

all._____ The win-ner takes it

267

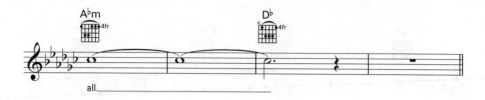

all.

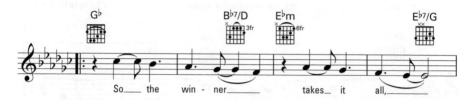

So__ the win - ner_____ takes__ it all,_____

Repeat to fade

and__ the los - er__ has__ to fall.___

Verse 2:
I was in your arms, thinking I belonged there
I figured it made sense building me a fence
Building me a home, thinking I'd be strong there
But I was a fool, playing by the rules
The gods may throw the dice, their minds as cold as ice
And someone way down here loses someone dear
The winner takes it all, the loser has to fall
It's simple and it's plain, why should I complain?

Verse 3:
But tell me, does she kiss like I used to kiss you?
Does it feel the same when she calls your name?
Somewhere deep inside, you must know I miss you
But what can I say? Rules must be obeyed
The judges will decide, the likes of me abide
Spectators of the show, always staying low
The game is on again: a lover or a friend
A big thing or a small, the winner takes it all.

Verse 4:
I don't wanna talk if it makes you feel sad
And I understand you've come to shake my hand
I apologise if it makes you feel bad
Seeing me so tense, no self-confidence.
The winner takes it all, the winner takes it all.

Wonderwall

Wonderwall was a quirky 1968 film perhaps most interesting for its musical score created by George Harrison. As such, its soundtrack album *Wonderwall Music* became technically the first solo Beatle LP although the film also featured contributions from Eric Clapton and a now-forgotten Liverpool group, The Remo Four. Decades later Beatles disciple Noel Gallagher picked up on it and wrote 'Wonderwall' for Oasis, giving the vocal honours to his brother Liam and chalking up a major hit for the band. The melody and Liam Gallagher's vocal together evoke something of the gritty energy and focus of a Lennon-driven Beatles song, perhaps one composed in the living room with voice and guitar before being taken to the studio for a full workout.

Wonderwall

Words & Music by Noel Gallagher

♩ = 158

Capo fret 3

1. To - day is gon-na be the day that they're gon-na throw it back to you._
(Verses 2 & 3 see block lyrics)

By now you should have some-how re - al - ised what you got - ta do_

I don't be-lieve_ that a - ny-bo - dy feels the way I do_

1.

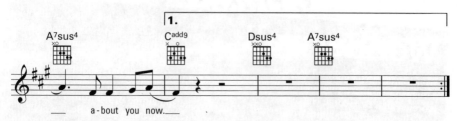

a-bout you now._

2, 3.

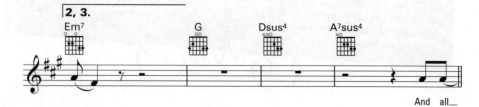

And all_

the roads we have__ to walk_ are wind - ing, and all_

the lights_ that lead__ the way are blind - ing.

There are ma - ny things__ that I____ would like to say to you__

__ but I don't know how._____ Be-cause

may - be_____ you're gon - na be the one that saves me,__

To Coda ⊕

__ and af - ter all_____ you're my

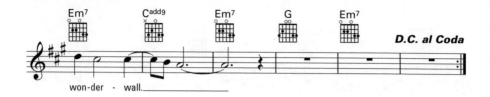

won-der - wall._____

You're gon - na be the one that saves me,_____

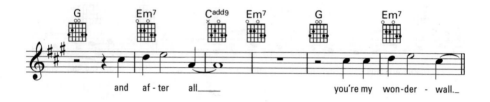

and af-ter all_____ you're my won-der - wall._

_____ You're my won-der - wall.

Verse 2:
Back beat, the word is on the street that the fire in your heart is out
I'm sure you've heard it all before but you never really had a doubt
I don't believe that anybody feels the way I do about you now.

Verse 3:
Today was gonna be the day, but they'll never throw it back to you
By now you should have somehow realised what you gotta do
I don't believe that anybody feels the way I do about you now.